HOW
TUTORING
WORKS

HOW TUTORING WORKS

WORKS

SIX STEPS TO GROW MOTIVATION & ACCELERATE STUDENT LEARNING

For
Tutors and
Teachers

NANCY FREY · DOUGLAS FISHER · JOHN ALMARODE

CORWIN
Fisher & Frey

FOR INFORMATION:

Corwin

A SAGE Company

2455 Teller Road

Thousand Oaks, California 91320

(800) 233-9936

www.corwin.com

SAGE Publications Ltd.

1 Oliver's Yard

55 City Road

London EC1Y 1SP

United Kingdom

SAGE Publications India Pvt. Ltd.

B 1/I 1 Mohan Cooperative Industrial Area

Mathura Road, New Delhi 110 044

India

SAGE Publications Asia-Pacific Pte. Ltd.

18 Cross Street #10-10/11/12

China Square Central

Singapore 048423

President: Mike Soules

Associate Vice President and
    Editorial Director: Monica Eckman

Director and Publisher, Corwin Classroom: Lisa Luedeke

Senior Content Development Manager: Julie Nemer

Associate Content Development Editor: Sharon Wu

Production Editor: Melanie Birdsall

Typesetter: C&M Digitals (P) Ltd.

Proofreader: Theresa Kay

Cover Designer: Gail Buschman

Marketing Manager: Deena Meyer

Printed in the United States of America

ISBN 978-1-0718-5595-9

Library of Congress Control Number: 2021909164

This book is printed on acid-free paper.

21 22 23 24 25 10 9 8 7 6 5 4 3 2 1

Contents

For additional resources, please visit
the companion website at
resources.corwin.com/howtutoringworks

Introduction

• •

"Is it my turn?" asks Jesse.

His teacher smiles. "No, not yet, but soon. Can you finish your brainstorm so you're ready?"

Jesse returns to his paper and reviews what he has already written. He begins to add words and phrases to the list already there. A few minutes later, the door opens, and another adult enters the room. Jesse looks up and smiles, knowing it's his turn. The adult nods and Jesse leaves his seat and walks to the door. As he approaches the adult, Jesse says, "Hi, Mr. Joe. I'm ready! I have a big list."

Joe Sacheverell is pleased and responds, "That's great, buddy. I can't wait to get started."

Mr. Sacheverell, or Mr. Joe, as the students call him, is a supplemental teacher who was hired to provide tutoring for students. Of course, tutoring can be provided by classroom teachers, paraprofessionals, and even volunteers who have been trained and supported to engage students in learning. In studies of tutoring, it's not simply the instructional knowledge that makes a difference. Yes, tutors need to know how to engage students in meaningful learning. But it's more than that. Tutors, whoever they are, need to be caring and work to establish a strong relationship with the students they tutor.

In studies of tutoring, it's not simply the instructional knowledge that makes a difference.

As Jesse and Mr. Joe walk outside, Mr. Joe asks Jesse about the Packers. "I know it's your team and all, but what about last night? What happened?" They engage in some banter about the players, the referee who made a bad call, and their hope for the next game. As they sit down at the table, Mr. Joe says, "So, now we have this writing assignment. The last time we talked, you told me that you were a bad writer. I don't see that. In fact, your opening sentence is pretty amazing."

Jesse responded, "Yeah, but it's just the first sentence. The rest of it kinda sucks. Oh, sorry."

1

"I get it. But you have a list of ideas, right? Now we have to figure out how to get your ideas out there. But before we do that, I just want to say that I think you've made a lot of progress on this. You've hooked the reader and you have a good organization already. We just need to focus on the details and your conclusion. It needs to have a punch, like that opening sentence. I think our goal today should be to add the details that you've been thinking about and edit the sentences a bit. We can work on the conclusion later. Agree?"

The session continues and Mr. Joe asks Jesse about the details that he has brainstormed and where they can be added to his draft. Mr. Joe also focuses on some sentence-level work that Jesse needs. Jesse writes with many fragments and run-on sentences. He also starts sentences with the same word and has little sentence variation.

Mr. Joe also asks Jesse to read his draft aloud, noting that "when you hear what you have written, sometimes it helps you make corrections yourself." At the end of their session, Mr. Joe asks Jesse to reflect on their time together. "How did this work for you? How are you feeling?"

"Well, I still have a lot to do, but I think it's better now. I think I get the part about run-ons with too many *and*s in the sentence and how to make them more sentences. I'm not sure about it when you say *fragments,* so I need more help with that. Oh, and I know how to start sentences with different words and make some shorter and some longer. Like you said, we gotta keep the reader with us. Do I see you tomorrow?"

> *Effective tutoring builds students'* confidence *and* competence.

Mr. Joe responds, "Yep. I get to see you tomorrow. Remember, you have some practice to do before I see you. Can you read it aloud to yourself and see if there are things that you'd like to change? And can you add details to the last two paragraphs like we did for the first ones?" Jesse agrees and they head back to the classroom.

A Model of Tutoring

Mr. Joe understands the power of tutoring and the ways in which his moves impact the learner. Tutoring is not just making sure that students complete their homework. And it's not just about telling students the information they are missing. Effective tutoring is much more complex than that and involves several strategic moves that build students' *confidence* and *competence*. Both are important in the tutoring situation, and we will devote an entire chapter to this issue. For now, let us recognize that we want to increase students' knowledge and skills, or their competence. But students who are receiving tutoring know that they have gaps in their learning and are sensitive to experiencing failure again and again. Thus, a significant focus of effective tutoring is in rebuilding students' confidence.

Our model of tutoring has six components. They are derived from research evidence about effective tutoring and interventions. Throughout this book, we will include effect sizes from Visible Learning® (www.visiblelearningmetax.com). This database is a collection of meta-analyses, or studies of studies. There are thousands of them, and the overall average impact on learning is an effect size of 0.40. Thus, anything that we report above the 0.40 effect size is an accelerator of learning. In terms of the tutoring components, all six are important, and missing any one of them places the student receiving the tutoring at risk. The six components include

1. **Establishing, nurturing, and repairing relationships.**
   To paraphrase the late Rita Pierson, "Young people do not learn from older people they do not like." The effect size of teacher credibility is 1.09. Relationships are especially important in the tutoring situation. Tutors work with students who have experienced failure, students who have difficulty learning and remembering, and students who have had ineffective instructional experiences. As we will see in Chapter 1, tutoring begins with establishing a healthy, growth-producing relationship. This is more than a getting-to-know-you phase; this relationship needs to be nurtured and grown. And sometimes, things happen that strain the relationship. Imagine studying with a tutor only to fail on an assessment. Naturally, the student will blame the tutor and the relationship will be fractured. Effective tutors recognize that this is part of the process and work to reestablish the relationship and, when they have done so, help the student identify what went wrong and how to address it in the future. Tutors do not blame students for their circumstances and display great empathy with the students they tutor.

All six tutoring components are important, and missing any one of them places the student receiving the tutoring at risk.

2. **Addressing confidence and challenges to learning.**
As you noted when you read about Mr. Joe and Jesse, there
was a lack of confidence on the part of the student. This is
not unusual. Students receiving tutoring typically recognize
that they are struggling. They know that they need help. Part
of the power of tutors is their ability to address confidence
issues as they arise. Given that tutoring is individual or small
group, tutors can recognize the signs of lack of confidence
and include confidence-building activities in each session.
Tutors can also be on the lookout for cognitive challenges
to learning, such as a student's mindset or limits to working
memory. Each of the common cognitive challenges to
learning has specific actions that tutors can take to address
those challenges. When students have high levels of efficacy,
they learn more. The effect size of self-efficacy is 0.71,
meaning that it holds the potential to accelerate learning.

3. **Setting goals.** Every single tutoring session should have a
goal. Tutors and students should talk about the goals they
have for the session and then reflect on those goals at the
end of the session. Of course, the goal is about learning
something. Having learning goals versus not having them
has an effect size of 0.51. It's key that students have a
mastery goal orientation rather than a performance goal
orientation. In other words, it's more valuable to say, "I want
to learn to write well" or "I want to use my writing to create
changes in the world" than to say, "I want to get an A on this
essay" or "I want to pass this class." When students have
goals, they are more likely to engage in the tutoring session
and to complete the practice tasks that are assigned to them.
When students seek help, meaning that they know where
they need help, the effect size is 0.72.

4. **Learning how to learn.** Many students who require
tutoring are unsure how to learn. They may possess
ineffective learning strategies, meaning that the effort
is there, but the result isn't. They may complete their
assignments, but they may not be learning much in the
process. Tutoring is an opportunity to help students learn
how to learn. Of course, students also need to learn content,
but the tutor (and teacher) are only with students for a

finite number of hours a day. If we can teach students how to learn, the impact increases as students begin to teach themselves. One of the ways to learn is study skills, with an effect size of 0.54. Figure I.1 presents a list of learning strategies and their effect sizes.

5. **Learning content.** This is the core of the tutoring session. The whole point of tutoring is to ensure that students learn more concepts and skills. The tutor needs to know the content well enough to guide students in their thinking without simply telling them answers. But knowing content, or teachers' subject matter knowledge, has a surprisingly low impact on students' learning, with an effect size of 0.23. That's probably because knowing *how* to teach that content is even more important. Our take on this influence is that you have to know the content and how to teach that content, or what is referred to as pedagogical content knowledge (Shulman, 1986). Of course, there is not a single "right" way to teach. There are a number of effective instructional approaches, depending on what students need to learn and where they are in their learning journey. But there are also bad choices in terms of instructional moves. What we care about is learning. As we will discuss in the chapter on learning content, the focus should be on whether the selected tools actually increased student learning. Knowing what success looks like and monitoring students' progress toward that success has an effect size of 0.88.

You have to know the content and how to teach that content, or what is referred to as pedagogical content knowledge (Shulman, 1986).

6. **Practicing deliberately.** Relationships and credibility, confidence, goals, and instruction are all important aspects of the tutoring experience. But if the learning is going to stick, students need to practice. Practice does not make perfect; practice makes permanent. The truth is that a lot of students in need of tutoring have had reasonably good instruction. They just didn't practice enough to ensure that the instruction had a chance to stick. Of course, there are students who have experienced instructional loss, reduced instructional minutes,

Figure I.1   Sample Learning Strategies

STRATEGY	DEFINITION	EFFECT SIZE
Outlining and summarizing	This practice involves identifying the main ideas and rendering them in one's own words. The core skill is being able to distinguish between the main ideas and the supporting ideas and examples.	0.66
Rereading	When students encounter difficulty in understanding, rereading aims to enhance meta-comprehension—enabling students to know better whether they have understood the text—and it can involve asking students to reread a passage with various purposes in mind.	0.53
Summarizing	The ability to summarize a text is often taken as a marker of reading comprehension, and for this reason many scholars have advocated explicit summarization training for students who struggle with comprehension. This can include deleting unnecessary material, deleting redundant material, substituting a subordinate term for a list of items or actions, selecting a topic sentence, and constructing a topic if one is only implicitly suggested by the text.	0.74
Annotating (underlining, highlighting, etc.)	This involves underlining or highlighting the main ideas, or how ideas are related, and aims to help the reader with recall and recognition of the links between parts of the text.	0.44
Note-taking	This involves students making notes in a systematic manner. Such note-taking has been linked to increased engagement, more generative learning, and greater self-efficacy. Of note, this is not sharing or providing students with notes, but the student learning the skills of note-taking.	0.51
Strategy monitoring	A metacognitive practice whereby a student monitors their own strategies to complete a task, this often involves students being trained both in problem-solving techniques and in monitoring techniques (through which they observe how and whether they are following problem-solving protocols).	0.58

Source: www.visiblelearningmetax.com

and ineffective instructional events. They also need practice aligned with good instruction. Two things are important here. First, the practice needs to be spaced out, not occurring all at once. In other words, the tutoring session is not just a pile o' practice. Distributed practice over time has an effect size of 0.65. Practice testing has an effect size of 0.46. And deliberate practice, which we will explore further in the last chapter of this book, has an effect size of 0.79. The overall effectiveness of our expanded opportunities to learn through tutoring is likely going to be dependent on whether we can get students to engage in practice.

Acceleration, Not Remediation

The worry we have in writing a book about tutoring is that we contribute to deficit thinking about students. The students who are assigned tutors have needs. And these needs are generally greater than the needs of other students in the school; thus, the allocation of resources for tutoring. In some places, the students receiving tutoring are labeled as the adults talk about them as a group. We've heard of the "Covidians" and the "DLVs (distance learning victims)" labels used to identify students receiving tutoring. In the past, this group might have been labeled the "ostriches" (birds that don't fly but run fast) or the "bubble kids" (students who need to pass a state exam). Not labeling students has an effect size of 0.61. Yes, that research comes from special education, but the point is well taken. When we label students, we run the risk of lowering our expectations for them.

Not labeling students has an effect size of 0.61.

And when we create these groups of students, we tend to focus on remediation of skills that have yet to be developed. As noted in Figure I.2, remediation slows down the learning and focuses on isolated skills. The lessons are not seen as relevant and instead the focus is on "catching up" with others. Acceleration, on the other hand, based on the research done with students identified as gifted (and yes, we recognize the label), suggests the opposite. The effect size of acceleration is 0.68, well worth the effort to change the focus. Acceleration does not mean skipping a grade level or covering two chapters in five minutes. Instead, acceleration and learning recovery means focusing on and ensuring that the core and

Figure I.2   Acceleration and Remediation: A Comparison

	ACCELERATION	REMEDIATION
Self-efficacy	▶ Self-confidence and engagement increase. ▶ Academic progress is evident.	▶ Students perceive they're in the "slow class," and self-confidence and engagement decrease. ▶ Backward movement leads to a sense of futility and lack of progress.
Basic skills	▶ Skills are hand-picked just in time for new concepts. ▶ Students apply skills immediately.	▶ Instruction attempts to reteach every missing skill. ▶ Skills are taught in isolation and not applied to current learning.
Prior knowledge	▶ Key prior knowledge is provided ahead of time, enabling students to connect to new information.	▶ Prior knowledge that connects to new learning is typically not introduced.
Relevance	▶ Relevance is treated as a critical component of student motivation and memory.	▶ Relevance is not seen as a priority.
Connection to core class	▶ Instruction is connected to core class; ongoing collaboration is emphasized.	▶ Instruction is typically isolated from the core class.
Pacing and direction	▶ The pacing and direction are active, fast-paced, hands-on. ▶ There is forward movement; the goal is for students to learn on time with peers.	▶ The pacing and direction are passive, with a focus on worksheets or basic software programs. ▶ There is backward movement; the goal is for students to catch up to peers.

Source: Rollins (2014).

key parts of the curriculum are covered and that they are covered with depth. In terms of the evidence on acceleration, several areas are important in creating these types of experiences for students. We'll highlight three of them here as they transcend the tutoring experience.

1. **Identify skills and concepts that have yet to be learned.** When you understand the skills and concepts that students are expected to master, you can identify which of these have yet to be learned. As Nuthall (2007) noted, about 40% of instructional minutes are spent on things that students already know. To accelerate learning, that number has to be much lower. Importantly, that 40% could differ from student to student. They all come to class (or to a tutoring session) knowing things. The problem is that some of them know this and others know that, so we tend to teach everything that anyone might need to learn. Obviously, that's not very effective and will not allow us to accelerate learning. Assessments provide information about what students have yet to learn. These assessments can be informal or more formal. But you need the data if you are going to accelerate learning. Think about the data the tutor needs to determine what students have already learned and what they still need to learn.

Research suggests that about 40% of instructional minutes are spent on things that students already know.

2. **Increase the relevance of students' learning.** When learning is relevant, students are more likely to allocate resources to learn. And by resources, we mean time and attention. The typical ways for increasing relevance include making connections beyond the walls of the classroom and providing students with opportunities to learn about themselves. For example, a tutor might note that this content will help them understand why it rains more in one place than another. Or the teacher might explain that this is an opportunity for them to understand how they solve problems and how their skills in problem

solving differ from others'. Generally, these still work to ensure that students find relevance in their learning. But the reality is that this aspect of learning is often neglected or rushed. There are far too many students who have no idea how to answer the question, "Why am I learning this?" And there are so many of us educators who aren't sure either. We need to seriously consider the reasons that students need to know or be able to do something and then explore that with students. When they accept the challenge of learning and see that learning as relevant, they are much more likely to learn. And that's acceleration. Before we leave the topic of relevance, we'd also like to note that your passion for students, their learning, and the content they are learning contributes to relevance. We can all remember a time that we learned something simply because the person teaching us was so excited. Bring that passion and excitement to your class or tutoring session and show students how amazing it feels to learn things. When we do, our students might just suspend their disbelief and engage with us on another level, opening the door for further acceleration.

3. **Create active, fast-paced learning experiences.** One of the norms with remediation is slowing down the learning and focusing on smaller and smaller aspects. Perhaps that's not always intended, but the trend in these types of efforts is to assume that students are far behind and need the pace to be slower so that they can learn. The opposite is true. Acceleration requires that we create active lessons in which students have multiple response opportunities. Remember, we're trying to build a memory trace through repetition and retrieval. The more often learners retrieve information, the more likely they are to remember it and be able to apply it.

When students accept the challenge of learning, and see that learning as relevant, they are much more likely to learn. And that's acceleration.

Build a Tutoring Program for Success

Tutors may be drawn from the credentialed teaching ranks, or they may be paraprofessionals. In other cases, tutors may be community volunteers. Whatever your level of experience, we want to acknowledge what it is that you need from a tutoring program. The first is that tutors should receive regular professional learning in order to refine skills and provide feedback to the school about the program. Tutors need (and deserve) to know the goals of the tutoring program, especially knowing that it is for the purpose of strengthening knowledge of concepts and skills, and not just providing homework help and passing classroom tests.

> *The more often learners retrieve information, the more likely they are to remember it and be able to apply it.*

Collaboration between teachers and tutors is crucial for aligning student experiences between the two settings. The evidence on collaboration between educators resoundingly notes that communication among adults about monitoring progress toward academic goals increases student learning. Collaboration should also happen with families, but who is the communicator? Is it the classroom teacher or the tutor? Again, these questions should be clarified in advance.

Tutors must have access to supportive instructional resources, including textbooks and other curricular materials. In addition, these materials should include supportive supplemental materials that support core texts. This extends to access to results of diagnostic assessments that have been completed. Ask as well about the responsibilities of tutors in conducting interim or benchmark assessments. Student progress should be monitored carefully and not solely constructed as a time-based project. Be sure to ask what the criteria are for discontinuing tutoring services when goals have been achieved.

Students who need specialized attention, especially those who qualify for special education services or 504 supports, deserve to have a coordinated network around them. When this is the case, ask for the student's applicable individualized goals, and speak regularly with the student's case manager. In addition, inquire about how best to report on progress so that this information is documented in the student's individualized education plan. In support of your efforts, Figure I.3 lists possible questions to ask as you move into a tutoring role.

Figure I.3   Questions to Ask About the Tutoring Program

TOPIC	QUESTIONS
Program goals	▶ What are the goals of the tutoring program? ▶ How does the tutoring program work in conjunction with classroom learning? ▶ How is the success of the program measured? ▶ How is the success of students measured? ▶ What is the supervision model for the tutoring program?
Collaboration	▶ How do tutors and classroom teachers collaborate and exchange information? Is there a designated time or channel for doing so? ▶ What are the best ways for me to access supports (e.g., coaching and supervision)?
Professional learning	▶ What are the initial onboarding and program training opportunities? ▶ How are tutors continuing their professional learning throughout the year?
Curriculum and materials	▶ What core curricular materials are available? ▶ What supportive supplemental materials are available? ▶ What modified materials are available for those students with IEPs (individualized education programs) who need them?
Communication	▶ Do tutors attend IEP and 504 meetings? ▶ Who are the individuals that should be included in electronic communications? ▶ How are families informed about tutoring progress?
Assessment	▶ How are the results of applicable standards-based assessments shared with tutors? ▶ How are the results of applicable diagnostic assessments shared with tutors? ▶ What are the benchmark, interim, or curricular assessment responsibilities of tutors?
Recordkeeping	▶ What are the documentation requirements of tutors? ▶ How is progress reported?

Conclusion

Extending learning and addressing the unrealized potential in students is the goal of tutoring. When we develop strong relationships, focus on students' confidence, establish shared goals, teach students well, and ensure that they practice, amazing things can happen. Most important, tutoring is a specialized skill set and differs from teaching the whole class or even small groups. With support, nearly anyone can be a tutor. Whether you are an educational specialist, resource teacher, classroom teacher, paraprofessional, or volunteer, you have the potential to impact students—specifically students who have a damaged relationship with learning. What a powerful role and responsibility. Be that person who makes a difference in the lives of young people; our future depends on it.

Effective Tutoring Begins With Relationships and Credibility

CHAPTER
1

. . . .

Imagine that you are a young person who hasn't experienced success in school. You've got a damaged relationship with learning and have doubts about your abilities. Now your school has said that because you haven't been making expected progress, you're going to be enrolled in additional tutoring. You have to show up for your first tutoring session. You don't know this person who'll be working with you. You're suspicious of the whole process and determined not to let your guard down.

It can be easy to consider tutoring primarily as an academic process. After all, the purpose is to accelerate learning by addressing knowledge gaps. But emotion and motivation are the fire under cognition. Failure to address the emotional and motivational dimensions of tutoring can mute its potential to accelerate academic learning. Educational researcher Robert Slavin notes that tutoring appears to be effective not only because of the precision that comes with tailoring lessons to meet individual needs; it is "individualization plus nurturing and attention" (2018, ¶ 8).

> *Emotion and motivation are the fire under cognition.*

When that young person enters your session for the first time, they may be wary, or fearful, or resentful, or enthusiastic. If you are a stranger to them, or someone they know only vaguely as a member of the school staff, they don't have a relationship with you. You also don't have any credibility with them. These two factors—the quality of the relationship and your perceived credibility—are key to the emotional and motivational dimensions of learning. In this chapter, we'll examine the role of relationships and credibility in tutoring. And we'll make some suggestions about how to use both when problems arise.

The Power of Relationships in Learning

Ask an educator what matters in learning and within moments they will be talking about the human connection. Effective tutors know one's students as individuals who have rich stories to tell and aspirations for their futures. These are the starting points of relationship building. Who did you learn best from? Likely it was a teacher with whom you had a positive relationship. Positive relationships between teachers and students form the heart of what Hattie and Zierer (2018) refer to as *mindframes* of educators:

1. I focus on learning and the language of learning.

2. I strive for challenge and not merely expecting students to "do their best."

3. I recognize that learning is hard work.

4. I build relationships and trust so that learning can occur in a place where it is safe to make mistakes and learn from others.

5. I engage as much in dialogue as in monologue.

6. I inform all about the language of learning.

7. I am a change agent and believe that all students can improve.

8. I give and help students to understand feedback and I interpret and act on feedback given to me.

9. I see assessment as informing my impact and next steps.

10. I collaborate with others.

Consider the extent to which the quality of the relationship between educator and learner underpins many of these mindframes. There is the social sensitivity needed to understand that learning is hard work and to never demean a student's efforts. The orientation to dialogic (rather than monologic) teaching suggests that the adult takes the student's ideas seriously. In doing so, it allows you to hear how and what that young person is thinking. These tutors know that feedback is about what is received, not what is given, and that a fraught relationship diminishes feedback's usefulness. And educators hold tight to a core assumption: they deeply believe that they can change the trajectory of a child's educational path and have evidence of their impact to do so.

Characteristics of Teacher-Student Relationships

People learn better when they have a positive relationship with the person providing instruction. The evidence of the influence of teacher-student relationships is a positive one, with an effect size of 0.48 (Hattie, 2018). The story behind the data speaks to its potential to accelerate achievement. Elements of teacher-student relationships include (Cornelius-White, 2007, p. 113):

▶ **Teacher empathy**—understanding

▶ **Unconditional positive regard**—warmth

▶ **Genuineness**—the teacher's self-awareness

▶ **Nondirectivity**—student-initiated and student-regulated activities

▶ **Encouragement of critical thinking** as opposed to traditional memory emphasis

These student-centered practices are essential in any setting, perhaps even more so in a tutoring session. Establishing these conditions begins from the first interactions students have with you.

▶ Strong teacher-student relationships rely on effective communication and a willingness to address issues that strain the relationship.

▶ Positive relationships are fostered and maintained when tutors set fair expectations and hold students accountable for the expectations in an equitable way.

▶ Importantly, relationships are not destroyed when problematic behaviors occur, either on the part of the tutor or the student. This is an important point for educators. If we want to ensure students read, write, communicate, and think at high levels, we have to develop positive, trusting relationships with *each* student.

Importantly, positive relationships build trust and make your tutoring sessions a safe place to explore what students do not know, including their errors and misconceptions. Indeed, powerful student-teacher relationships allow errors to be seen as opportunities to learn.

A lot of students avoid situations where they are likely to make errors or expose their lack of knowledge. But we want to turn these situations into powerful learning opportunities, and this is more likely to occur in high-trust environments. Figure 1.1 is a list on building teacher-student relationships we have started for you. Customize it to fit your context.

> *Positive relationships build trust and make your tutoring sessions a safe place to explore what students do not know.*

Figure 1.1 Building Relationships With Students

How will you establish (or reestablish) relationships with students in your tutoring sessions? We've started a list for you. How will you personalize it to your context?	
Teacher empathy *How do you learn about your student?*	▶ Ask open-ended questions about their lives ("What kind of things do people ask you for help with?"). ▶ Engage in active listening of your student. ▶ Host short check-in conferences with families and the student to see how they are doing and what they need.
Unconditional positive regard *How do your students know you care about them as people?*	▶ Weave into lessons what you have learned about the student's pursuits. ▶ Match your praise with evidence ("Do you see my grin? It's because you noticed that error on your own and fixed it without my saying anything"). ▶ Use voice feedback tools on student work so they can hear the sparkle in your voice, rather than read your words without context.
Genuineness *How do your students know that you care about yourself as a professional?*	▶ Dress and groom professionally. ▶ Project a demeanor that is optimistic about them and you. ▶ Make it clear in words and actions that this is a place for learning about themselves and the world.

Nondirectivity *How do your students know you hold their abilities in high regard?*	▶ Hold conversations with the student to help them identify their strengths, goals, and growth areas. ▶ Ask questions that mediate the student's thinking, rather than asking leading questions. ▶ Help the student clarify their ideas by restating and paraphrasing.
Encouragement of critical thinking *How do your students know that they are capable?*	▶ Foster discussion using questions that open up their thinking. ▶ Every session should include opportunities for the student to write about, illustrate, or discuss their thinking, not just complete tasks. ▶ Ask them reflective questions designed to foster metacognition ("What was hard about this lesson? What were you successful at accomplishing?").

Positive teacher-student relationships are necessary conditions for learning to occur. They allow the student to let their guard down and open themselves up to the risk-taking needed to engage with content they aren't feeling very good about. A positive relationship sets the table for learning. Tutors and their students should have healthy, growth-producing relationships, in part because students learn more when these conditions are present. It's hard to imagine that a tutor could be credible with students without a strong relationship. At the basic level, tutors need to be seen as believable, convincing, and capable of persuading students that they can be successful. But it isn't the whole meal. A student can have a perfectly pleasant relationship with a tutor but not learn much of anything. Your credibility plays a significant role.

Teacher Credibility

Do your students believe that they can learn from you? If your answer is yes, it is likely that they will learn a lot more. The effect size of teacher credibility, which is the label we give to the concept that students believe that they can learn from their teachers, is 1.09. *Wow*, right? It's powerful. But, like all the influences that are likely to significantly accelerate learning, it's hard to accomplish. The credibility a tutor has with their students changes; it's dynamic. It's not the same for all students at the same time. As we have previously noted, "The dynamic of teacher credibility is always in play" (Fisher et al., 2016, p. 10). And here's the rub: we don't get to decide if we're credible. It is perceptual, on the part of the learner. *They* decide if we are credible.

Teacher credibility is a measure of the student's belief that you are trustworthy, competent, dynamic, and approachable. Thankfully, there are specific actions that tutors can take to increase their credibility in each of these four areas (Fisher et al., 2020). You'll note the role of positive relationships in three of these.

> *Teacher credibility is a measure of the student's belief that you are trustworthy, competent, dynamic, and approachable.*

Trust

Students need to know that their tutors care about them as individuals and have their best academic and social interests at heart. Students also want to know that their tutor is true to their word and is reliable. A few points about trust:

▶ If you make a promise, work to keep it (or explain why you could not).

▶ Tell students the truth about their performance (they know when their work is below standard and wonder why you are telling them otherwise).

▶ Don't spend all of your time trying to catch students in the wrong (and yet be honest about the impact that their behavior has on you as an individual).

▶ Examine any negative feelings you have about specific students (they sense it, and it compromises the trust within the classroom).

But there are additional considerations. Hoy and Tschannen-Moran identified five elements for trust to be developed and maintained, including (as defined by von Frank, 2010):

▶ **Benevolence:** Confidence that one's well-being or something one cares about will be protected by the trusted party . . . the assurance that others will not exploit one's vulnerability or take advantage even when the opportunity is available

▶ **Honesty:** The trusted person's character, integrity, and authenticity . . . acceptance of responsibility for one's actions and not distorting the truth in order to shift blame to another

▶ **Openness:** The extent to which relevant information is shared . . . openness signals reciprocal trust

▶ **Reliability:** Consistency of behavior and knowing what to expect from others . . . a sense of confidence that one's needs will be met in positive ways

▶ **Competency:** The ability to perform as expected and according to standards appropriate to the task at hand (p. 2)

Taken together, these dimensions of trust are your tutoring currency. Your consistent demonstration of these factors contributes to your ability to positively influence the learner as a believable source.

Competence

In addition to trust, students want to know that their tutor knows their stuff and knows how to teach that stuff. They expect an appropriate level of expertise and accuracy. Further, students measure competence by the ability of the tutor to deliver instruction that is coherent and organized. They expect that lessons are well paced and the information is accurate.

1. Make sure you know the content well and be honest when a question arises that you are not sure about (this requires planning in advance).

2. Organize lesson delivery in a cohesive and coherent way.

3. Consider your nonverbal behaviors that communicate competence, such as the position of your hands when you talk with students or the facial expressions you make (students notice defensive positions, and nonverbal indications that they are not valued when they speak).

Dynamism

This dimension of teacher credibility focuses on the passion adults bring to the classroom and the content. It is really about your ability to communicate enthusiasm for your subject and your students. And it's about developing spirited lessons that capture students' interest. To improve dynamism,

1. **Rekindle your passion for the content you teach by focusing on the aspects that got you excited as a student.** Remember why you wanted to be a tutor and the content you wanted to introduce to your students. Students notice when their tutors are bored by the content and when the adult isn't really interested in the topic. We think that a tutor's motto should be "Make content interesting!"

2. **Consider the relevance of your lessons.** Does the content lend itself to application outside the classroom? Do students have opportunities to learn about themselves and their problem solving? Does the content help them become civic-minded and engaged in the community? Does it connect to universal human experiences, or ask students to grapple with ethical concerns? When there isn't relevance, students check out and may be compliant learners rather than committed learners.

> *We think that a tutor's motto should be "Make content interesting!"*

3. **Seek feedback from trusted colleagues about your lesson delivery.** Ask peers to sit in on a tutoring session to focus on the energy you bring and the impact on students' demeanors. Students respond to the passion and energy in a lesson, even if they didn't initially think they would be interested.

Immediacy

This final construct of teacher credibility focuses on accessibility and relatability as perceived by students. The concept of immediacy was introduced by social psychologist Albert Mehrabian (1971), who noted that "people are drawn toward persons and things they like, evaluate highly, and prefer; and they avoid or move away from things they dislike, evaluate negatively, or do not prefer" (p. 1). The effect size for immediacy is 0.66. A warm greeting matters, as does using the student's name during your sessions. Your nonverbal signals, including facial expressions and body language, should convey optimism and warmth. Tutors need to be accessible, and yet there needs to be a sense of urgency that signals to students that their learning is important to you.

1. Get to know something personal about each student, as students know when you don't know their names or anything about them.

2. Teach with urgency but not to the point that it is causing undo stress for them. That said, students want to know that their learning matters and that you are not wasting their time.

3. Start the session on time and use every minute wisely. Students notice when time is wasted. Have your materials ready to go.

Consider the following examples of general things you can do to ensure that your students feel close to you:

▶ Gesture when talking.

▶ Look at the student and smile while talking.

▶ Invite the student to provide feedback.

▶ Use vocal variety (pauses, inflections, stress, emphasis) when talking.

A student's perception of a teacher's credibility is a strong influence on a student's belief that they can learn (Won et al., 2017). Given that students being tutored may already have a damaged belief in their capacity to learn, one's credibility is a crucial tool in changing their internal narrative.

Recovering a Relationship When There Is Conflict

Not all students are thrilled to be tutored. They may have negative feelings about themselves or of schooling in general. These negative student perceptions can prompt problematic behavior that interferes with the learning. Affective statements are used to shift the language of adults when there is conflict in order to open a dialogue with a student. These are sometimes called "I" statements and are intended to label the feelings and emotions of the speaker, rather than to assign motivation and blame to the student. "You" statements often devolve into an accusatory tone and can stop the interaction before it has even begun. Carl Rogers, who pioneered nondirective therapy, believed that power was often used to shut down conversations. Thomas Gordon, a student of Dr. Rogers, developed "I" messages to build empathetic listening and reflective thinking. Gordon (2003) incorporated these into a teacher effectiveness training program as a means for educators to interact constructively with students. Affective statements further move students forward by linking these "I" messages to needs and requests.

Affective statements are a cornerstone of restorative practices, an alternative approach to classroom and school discipline that encourages students to form emotional bonds with adults while minimizing negative interactions (Costello et al., 2009). These statements draw on affect theory, which seeks to link actions to the emotions that drive them. Well-being and satisfaction result when emotions are positive or neutral, while anger, distress, or shame result from negative emotions (Tomkins, 1962). Affective statements are used to reduce negative emotions and restore positive and neutral emotions so that the student can reintegrate into the flow of learning. These provide a way for you to share with the student that you are frustrated not with them as a person but with the actions they have taken, allowing you to separate the deed and the doer. Students will often respond with an apology or by saying, "I didn't mean for you to feel that way." In addition, this provides space for the student to engage in reflection and positive action, rather than expending their energy on being defensive.

Too many students are approached with an accusatory tone of blame and anticipate punishment.

We have too many examples of students who are approached with an accusatory tone of blame and anticipate punishment. The student's immediate response is a wave of negative emotions and defensiveness that can trigger an escalation of the problematic behavior. For example, when a student is not engaged or is off task, a conventional response might be to tell the student to "pay attention."

But this does not allow the student to understand how their actions are affecting others or what the reason is for the expected behavior. The student knows only that they have been called out. Affective statements are a tool that tutors can use when minor conflict arises with a student. The original frame for Gordon's (2003) "I" messages was mostly to formulate a statement that focused on how the teacher was perceiving the conflict:

▶ **Give a short description of the problem behavior, without assigning blame.** ("I noticed you weren't paying much attention to me when I was teaching the last problem.")

▶ **Share the feelings it caused you to experience as a result of the problem behavior.** ("I felt disappointed in myself because I wasn't successful with you.")

▶ **Name the tangible effects the action had on you.** ("I'm concerned that I'll have to teach it again when you get stuck trying to do it alone.")

Affective statements build on these "I" messages by adding two more steps—a statement of need and a plan or request:

▶ **Name what you value and need.** ("It's important to me that we work together.")

▶ **State the plan or request.** ("Can you give me your attention for this next problem so that I can make sure you're getting the information you need to be successful?")

The addition of these last two steps shifts the student to redirection and a path for success while reducing the negative emotions that might otherwise interfere with getting the student back on track. This simple change can be a step toward building a relationship because you are now talking *with* the student rather than talking *at* them.

An initial challenge is properly labeling one's feelings in ways that are developmentally appropriate. Face it—as educators, we have been receiving on-the-job training since we were five years old. We have absorbed the ways our own teachers responded when they had a dust-up with a student. These responses are deeply engrained and not easily changed just by reading about affective statements.

Consider the following situations:

▶ A student is not engaged in the tutoring session. How do you redirect them using an affective statement?

▶ A student is horsing around with some classmates instead of coming to the tutoring session. How do you fix the situation using an affective statement?

▶ A student will not get off their smartphone during the tutoring session. How do you use an affective statement so that they will put it away?

Figure 1.2 provides some example sentence starters and responses to these scenarios.

Figure 1.2 Sentence Starters for Redirection

SCENARIO	SENTENCE STARTERS	SAMPLE RESPONSES
A student is not engaged in the tutoring session. How do you redirect them using an affective statement?	▶ I am so sorry that . . . ▶ I am concerned that . . . ▶ I am feeling frustrated about/ by/to see/to hear . . .	▶ I am so sorry that this lesson is not capturing your attention right now. Is there anything that I should know? ▶ I am concerned that you are going to miss some important information. How will I know that you are comfortable with the information? ▶ I am feeling frustrated to see you check out. I tried to make a really interesting lesson. I worked on it last night.

SCENARIO	SENTENCE STARTERS	SAMPLE RESPONSES
A student is horsing around with some classmates instead of coming to the tutoring session. How do you fix the situation using an affective statement?	▶ I am having a hard time understanding . . . ▶ I am so pleased by/to see/to hear . . . ▶ I am uncomfortable when I see/hear . . .	▶ I am having a hard time understanding what happened. I was worried about you. ▶ I am so pleased to see that you are ready to join me. I missed you. ▶ I am uncomfortable when I see you playing like that because I worry that you will get hurt. I know you like to play with friends, but I like it better when that is outside because it makes me less worried.
A student will not get off their smartphone. How do you use an affective statement so that they will put it away?	▶ I am uneasy about . . . ▶ I am concerned about . . . ▶ I am so thankful that/for . . .	▶ I am uneasy about your time on the phone. I am worried that there is something wrong because that is not the norm for you. ▶ I am concerned about your phone use. I see that it's increasing, and I worry that you won't remember all the information. How can I help? ▶ I am so thankful you are finishing up with your phone. I appreciate your responding to my request to put your phone away.

Conclusion

Many discussions about tutoring begin and end with determinations about the content to be taught. Mind you, that's important, and we'll address that soon. But the thread that runs through every tutoring session is the continuous investment in relationships and credibility. Unfortunately, these two factors are assumed to be in place and therefore are rarely addressed, even though they exert tremendous influence on whether the tutoring initiative will be successful. Your attention to these dimensions of learning helps to ensure that the nurturing and positive regard that fuel motivation is ever present. You are seen as a valued adult who recognizes their successes, and you are there for them even when they are not being their best selves.

Building Confidence and Addressing Challenges to Learning

As we have noted, confidence and competence are connected. But too often, tutors focus on students' *competence* and not their *confidence* to learn. Educators can build students' confidence in myriad ways. First, we are trustworthy, and we provide honest growth-producing feedback. Thus, students come to understand that we have their best interests at heart and care deeply about their learning. In addition, we refrain from overcorrecting. We listen, noting errors and misconceptions that we can address later, but we don't keep correcting students as it can compromise their confidence, which can lead to shutting down.

When students tell us that they can't do something, we add "... *yet*" and project the expectation that with additional learning, they will be able to accomplish great things. We're not suggesting that we falsely praise students or inflate their sense of current learning, but rather that we recognize that learning is a journey and that errors are opportunities to learn. Remember, confidence is based on experience, and educators can shape the current experiences that students have so that they tell a different story about themselves as they build the expectations they have for their own learning.

> *When students tell us that they can't do something, we add "... yet."*

The story students tell themselves about their learning lives is their self-concept, which has an effect size of 0.47. *Self-concept* is generally thought of as our perception of our behavior, abilities, and characteristics, or the mental picture of who one is as a person. Part of a student's overall self-concept relates to learning. Lizzy, for example, is an amazing skateboarder but does not define herself as an academic success. Her self-concept includes both her ability and her perceived weakness. Bracken (1996) suggested that there are six domains related to self-concept:

- **Academic:** Success or failure in school

- **Affect:** The awareness of emotional states

- **Competence:** The ability to meet basic needs

- **Family:** How well one functions within the family unit

- **Physical:** Feelings about looks, health, physical condition, and overall appearance

- **Social:** The ability to interact with others

Humanist psychologist Carl Rogers believed that there were three different parts of self-concept (1959):

- **Self-image**, or how you see yourself. Each individual's self-image is a mixture of different attributes, including our physical characteristics, personality traits, and social roles. Self-image doesn't necessarily coincide with reality. Some people might have an inflated self-image, while others may perceive or exaggerate the flaws and weaknesses that others don't see.

- **Self-esteem**, or how much you value yourself. Several factors can impact self-esteem, including how we compare ourselves to others and how others respond to us. When people respond positively to our behavior, we are more likely to develop positive self-esteem. When we compare ourselves to others and find ourselves lacking, we are likely to experience a negative impact on our self-esteem.

- **Ideal self,** or how you wish you could be. In many cases, the way we see ourselves and how we would like to see ourselves do not quite match up.

Tutors, using this knowledge, can modify a student's self-concept and show them that they are learning. Figure 2.1 contains a list of recommendations for parents. As you read through the recommendations, consider how many of them would also apply in a tutoring situation. Note that there is a focus on relationships, which we discussed in the last chapter. And note that there is a need to focus on strengths and show them that you believe that they can accomplish the goals you have agreed upon.

Figure 2.1 Ten Ways to Nurture Your Child's Self-Concept

1. **Be mindful of the language you use to describe your children.** Do not label them with negative terminology such as *lazy, hyper, aggressive,* or *mean.* Instead, actively look for and notice your child's strengths.

2. **Provide them with opportunities for success.** Give your child age-appropriate tasks they can complete on their own. This will give them a sense of accomplishment and help build a "can-do" mentality.

3. **Show your children that you have faith in their goodness and their abilities.** This is a matter of language choice. For example, if your toddler, out of frustration, hits another child, you might say, "How can you be so mean? I can't believe you hit them! You're in big trouble!" Or you could say, "You got frustrated, and we all feel like that sometimes. I know you didn't mean to hurt them, but hitting is not okay. Next time you can call for me or hit the pillow instead."

4. **Spend quality time together.** A vital part of having a healthy self-concept is feeling loved and valued. Spend this time doing something fun for both of you and avoid any criticism of behavior during this special time.

5. **Support your child's interests.** Learn what your child is interested in and support them in mastering that skill or accomplishing a desired level of achievement. Feeling competent and good at something grows a positive self-concept.

6. **Set reasonable rules and enforce them with loving kindness.** Your rules should be age-appropriate and clear. These help your child to feel safe and learn how to manage themselves. However, enforcing them with a heavy hand when your child steps out of bounds can erode the self-concept. It's important to make sure your child knows that making mistakes is a part of life and doesn't mean they're a bad person. When giving consequences, keep your child's dignity in mind.

(Continued)

(Continued)

---

7. **Help your child to manage their emotions and work out problems.** Encouraging problem solving is a big part of positive parenting. When children learn to solve their own problems, they build confidence and, therefore, a positive self-concept. Learning to manage emotions is key to having the ability to step back from a situation and view it objectively.

8. **Maintain a connected relationship.** Being connected keeps the lines of communication open, and this is especially important as your child grows into adolescence. Knowing that they have you to talk to, that you will listen without judgment and take their feelings seriously, will help them to feel supported, safe, and important.

9. **Give children the opportunity to explore their environment, ask questions without feeling like a nuisance, and engage in make-believe play activities.** Children are curious and imaginative, and we must be careful not to squash those traits. Nurture these traits in your children by allowing ample time for free play and exploration.

10. **Acknowledge effort and offer encouragement.** Your child needs to know that winning isn't the goal, but that doing their personal best is the most important, no matter what place that lands them. As they grow, their self-evaluation will become important to their self-concept, and they will learn to emphasize their strengths and accomplishments, even if there is no trophy in the end.

Source: Adapted from CALM (n.d.), Eanes (n.d.).

Strength-Spotting

As you engage with students in a tutoring session, ask yourself, *How can I learn to be a strength-spotter rather than a deficit-describer?* We recognize that students have areas of need that must be addressed. But they also have strengths and you should feel very comfortable talking about students' strengths. Doing so will build your relationship with the student and allow you to build on those strengths rather than begin lessons from a place of deficit. A few examples are in order:

▶ Tutor Marlow Jessop starts each lesson with a log entry. The students can identify a compliment they received, note something they are good at, or describe how they helped someone else. The student records this in their journal and they have a brief conversation about the strength before identifying the goal for the learning that day. Marisa wrote in her log that she was complimented for her illustration. Ms. Jessop asked for some details about the illustration, learning that it was part of a report she had done. Ms. Jessop said, "I love it. Maybe we'll add some illustrations to our work as we finish today."

> *How can I learn to be a strength-spotter*
> *rather than a deficit-describer?*

▶ Tutor Brad Green asks the teacher to create a list of strengths for each student who will be receiving tutoring on a given day. As Mr. Green starts the tutoring session, he lets the student know about their strengths. As he and Malik got to work, Mr. Green said, "So, I hear that you aced the math test. But even more than that, I hear that you were able to explain two of the tasks to your group and they got it because of you. How's that feel?"

▶ Tutor Naimo Amal ends her session listing the students' strengths that she observed during the small group lesson. These include academic as well as social and emotional strengths that the students displayed. Ms. Amal said to Arif, "You listened so carefully today. I could tell you were thinking about the ideas."

Take this to heart. To be an effective tutor, you should not limit your focus to areas of need. Yes, we need to close the gap between what students currently know and are able to do and what they need to know and be able to do, but starting with strengths and recognizing success goes a long way toward ensuring learning.

Building Confidence

We took a necessary detour to self-concept because tutors have the potential to shape the way students see themselves as learners. Tutors can also directly support students in building their confidence. A summary of ideas for building confidence can be found in Figure 2.2. We'll explore each of these further with examples from tutors who are making it happen.

Figure 2.2 Ways to Build Student Confidence

APPROACH	EXPLANATION
Set goals together	One of the most effective ways of building student confidence is making sure everyone is on the same page about learning goals. There is value in having clear learning intentions and success criteria. To build confidence, students and tutors need to understand and agree on the goals for learning.
Encourage self-assessment	A huge step toward building student confidence is in providing students opportunities to improve learning by encouraging ownership of this learning. When students learn to self-assess, the role of the teacher becomes to validate and challenge, rather than to decide if students have learned. When we do this, student understanding, ownership, enthusiasm for learning, and, of course, confidence, increase.
Give useful feedback	Feedback should make someone feel good about where they are and get them excited about where they can go. This is the exact mindset that develops as we continue building our learners' confidence in the classroom.
Empty their heads	Students tend to lose confidence in themselves because they feel they're struggling more than they are. Every once in a while, we've got to get learners to unpack everything in their heads through review and open discussion to show them just how much they've accomplished.
Show that effort is normal	Nothing kills confidence more than for a student to think they're the only one in class that doesn't understand something. Focus on the effort that everyone is making. A good way of building student confidence in such a case is by having that struggling student pair up with one of the others who has aced the topic and get them to explain it.
Celebrate success	Any kind of success in learning, no matter how big or small, deserves to be acknowledged and celebrated. This might mean more to some students than to others, but it's still a great way of building student confidence.

Source: Adapted from Wabisabi Learning (n.d.).

Set Goals Together

The task or assignment is likely given by the teacher. The skills and concepts that students still need to learn are likely identified on some sort of assessment. In other words, there is much that is already a given in a tutoring session. But what we can accomplish together can be discussed and agreed on. When students know what success looks like, they are more likely to allocate resources (time, attention, etc.) to learning. The effect size of having learning goals is 0.51.

Tutor Hayley Thibodeau asks her students what their goals are for the session. For example, Mikel said that he needed to understand the properties of matter. Ms. Thibodeau also proposes goals for students as she did with Mikel when she suggested that another goal for their time together might be to read informational texts, take notes, and retell the information to show understanding. Mikel agreed that he could do that as well.

Tutor Debra Ramirez was tutoring Ayub, who had difficulty with number sense. He did not have a complete understanding of one-to-one correspondence when counting that would lead to him adding numbers when there was not an item to be counted.

Ms. Ramirez asked Ayub what he wanted to learn, based on the numbers they had been focused on. Ayub said, "I want to count better."

Ms. Ramirez responded, "You are so good at keeping the numbers in order. You don't skip numbers. I agree that we can work on counting items. This time, let's move them to this circle [drawn on a personal dry erase board] when we count them."

Encourage Self-Assessment

When students understand what success looks like and are provided opportunities to assess their performance against those success criteria, they learn to monitor their progress and make adjustments to their learning (which could include attention, effort, strategies, etc.). Assessment of learning has an effect size of 0.64. Tutors can provide students with time to assess their own learning and discuss how they know that they have learned. Tutor Josiah Anderson was tutoring Miriam, who had not yet mastered sound-symbol correspondence. As part of the lesson, Mr. Anderson provided Miriam a stack of cards with various onset and rime words containing familiar patterns. Mr. Anderson asked Miriam to self-assess which words she could read and which ones were still hard for her. Miriam created a pile of words that she believed that she could read and read them to Mr. Anderson. Mr. Anderson then reviewed the pile that Miriam self-assessed that she could not read and noted that several of the words had a silent *e* at the end (e.g., *kite, bike, side*). He knew that he needed to provide her with additional instruction in this area.

> *Tutors can provide students with time to assess their own learning and discuss how they know that they have learned.*

Drew and Taryn were working with their tutor Michelle Leone as they focused on the ways in which a poem's structure or format influences the meaning. Ms. Leone asked the two students to create know/show charts about what they understood about the learning. In one column, students list all the things that they know relative to the success criteria. In the right column, they list all the ways that they can show what they know. In this case, Ms. Leone had her two students compare their "know" columns and tutor each other.

Give Useful Feedback

There are four types of feedback (Hattie & Timperley, 2007):

- Task-related
- Process-related
- Self-regulation-related
- Feedback about the person

Feedback has an effect size of 0.64. Corrective feedback about the task (*correct/not correct*) has a limited potential to motivate. When we grade a math assignment by marking which items are correct and which are not, we are not providing feedback. Novice tutors often focus on corrective feedback and thus have a limited impact on students' learning. Feedback about the person is also of limited usefulness. The effects of "Nice job" dissipate pretty quickly. Figure 2.3 provides an overview of the types of feedback as well as examples. We'd like to make a note about praise. Please feel free to praise the students you are tutoring. They appreciate it and it builds the connection you have with students. At the same time, recognize that it's not feedback for their learning. You can use the other types of feedback to ensure that the students you tutor are learning.

Figure 2.3   Types of Feedback

TYPE OF FEEDBACK	EXAMPLES	EFFECTIVENESS?
About the task (corrective feedback)	"You forgot a word here." "Number 17 is wrong." "You spelled these words incorrectly." "You need to focus."	Effective for feedback about mistakes in content learning; inadequate when the learner lacks knowledge or skill. Not very useful when used for behavior corrections
About the processing of the task	"I noticed that you focused on this task for twelve minutes without giving up or becoming distracted." "Did you notice how much more you learned when you were practicing your active listening strategies?"	Very effective, as it labels cognitive and metacognitive strategies the learner is using or should be using
About self-regulation	"I saw you were frustrated with number 17 and you decided to take a breath, try number 18 and then come back to 17." "I noticed that you decided to draw a little illustration on the side of the page when you got stuck. It seemed to work for you. Can you tell me more?"	Very effective, as it helps learners to self-assess their ability, actions, and knowledge
About the person	"Well done." "You did a good job." "You are such a good kid."	Ineffective, because it doesn't yield task-specific information

Empty Their Heads

Sometimes, students believe that they are struggling more than they are. They have told themselves that they can't do something or that they are incapable of learning the content. In these cases, the student does not recognize the parts that they have already mastered or the aspects that they already understand. To build students' confidence, you may need to have a frank conversation with them about where they struggle and where they have experienced success. Tutor Juan Torres did just that with Hector, who believed he could never add and subtract fractions. As Hector said, "I'm too stupid to do this. I don't get it. It's too hard for me."

Mr. Torres asked Hector to show him the last problem he was working on. Looking at the paper for a minute, Mr. Torres said, "Well, look at that. You have added the top numbers correctly: $\frac{4}{7}$ plus $\frac{1}{7}$ is what we're asked to figure out, right? You added the top numbers and got 5. Let's check the other problems to see if you got them right as well. Can you show me?"

Looking over Hector's work, Mr. Torres said, "You should feel good about this. On every one of these, you have the top number correct. You added them all and I can see that they are right. Your mind understands that, right?"

Hector agreed, but said, "But they are still wrong. Why?" Mr. Torres responded, "Well, let's look at the answer to see one of them so we can figure this out. The book says that $\frac{4}{7}$ plus $\frac{1}{7}$ is $\frac{5}{7}$." Hector responded, "But it should be $\frac{5}{14}$ because you have to add." Their conversation continued with Mr. Torres creating a visual to explain fractions and denominators. The point here is that Mr. Torres showed Hector what he was already doing well and then scaffolded the learning so that Hector could experience success.

Show That Effort Is Normal

In some cases, students believe that they are the only one who is struggling. They compare themselves to others, at least from the public perspective of others. It is rare for students to recognize that others also struggle and that the errors are opportunities to learn. Instead, they see the outward behaviors of their peers and believe that everyone, except them, understands. This is complicated by the fact that the student who believes that they are the only one who struggles is receiving tutoring. When this is the case, students need to know that effort is a natural part of the learning process and that others struggle as well. Some people have more effective learning strategies (which we will discuss in the next section) and others have more stamina. Regardless, if students come to understand that effort is required for learning to occur, they will be less dependent on tutors in the future.

> *Students need to know that effort is a natural part of the learning process and that others struggle as well.*

Tutor Anne Davis was working with Nicole, who asked why she didn't get it and why it was so easy for others in her class. Ms. Davis explained that everyone puts forth effort and that it was natural to feel a little frustrated when learning was hard. Ms. Davis told Nicole a personal story about a college class that she took and how it was so hard that she almost quit, thinking that she was the only one.

"But you're so smart," Nicole said.

"That's kind of you to say," Ms. Davis responded, "but I needed to learn that I had to try. I had to focus. I had to practice. And I had to accept the fact that some things are hard for me to learn."

Celebrate Success

Success is motivating. When students fail and fail again, it's demotivating. After all, who wants to spend lots of time failing? Most of us will eventually give up if we keep experiencing failure. When we experience success, we want to feel it again and again. It's rewarding. Many students receiving tutoring have histories of failure and very few celebrations of success. We're not talking about false praise, but rather recognition of the success that students have. At first, these successes may seem small. But, if you acknowledge and celebrate the actions and behaviors you want to see in the future, they are likely to be repeated. Over time, the recognition can be focused on bigger and bigger accomplishments.

Tutor Bryan Shin had to start small with Rick. Rick did not participate in school much for a year and had several gaps in his learning. Rick also had some skills. When Rick was able to work through an entire task, which took about ten minutes, Mr. Shin celebrated. When

Rick was able to complete the practice on his own, Mr. Shin celebrated. When Rick got his essay back with many positive comments, Mr. Shin celebrated. When Rick got his first A ever, Mr. Shin celebrated. And yes, we recognize that an A is performance and not mastery, but given that it was a first for Rick, it seemed worthy of celebration. As part of that celebration, Mr. Shin focused on all the things Rick had learned to earn that A.

Cognitive Challenges to Learning

It's easy to think that learning is as simple as introducing students to ideas and getting them to practice using those ideas. Learning is much more complicated than enacting good practices, in part because it is often interrupted by a range of challenges that students have experienced. Further, it is rarely linear, with students adding incrementally to what they begin with. It is more up-and-down, a staccato, where failure needs to be a learner's best friend, and it sometimes happens in an "aha" moment. Too often, we point our fingers at students' home lives or believe that students lack motivation, parental support, or innate abilities. Often, we point to things over which we have little control and instead simply admire the problem, while absolving ourselves of locating solutions. The reality is that students do experience cognitive challenges to their learning. But equally important is the fact that there are actions educators can take to reduce the impact that those challenges have.

> *Too often, we point our fingers at students'*
> *home lives or believe that students lack motivation,*
> *parental support, or innate abilities.*

Note that we are focused on cognitive challenges. As Chew and Cerbin (2020) found, "A cognitive challenge is a characteristic or aspect of mental processing that can affect the success or failure of learning" (p. 3). Based on their review of research, nine common cognitive challenges have been identified (see Figure 2.4). Note that there are specific actions that educators can take to address these cognitive challenges.

Figure 2.4 The Cognitive Challenges of Effective Teaching

CHALLENGE	DESCRIPTION
Student mental mindset	▶ Students hold attitudes and beliefs about a course or topic, such as how interesting or valuable it will be and how capable they are to master it through their own efforts. ▶ Students may believe a course is irrelevant to them or that they lack the ability needed to learn the content.
Metacognition and self-regulation	▶ Students monitor and judge their level of understanding of concepts and they regulate their learning behaviors to achieve a desired level of mastery. ▶ Students may be overconfident in their level of understanding.
Student fear and mistrust	▶ Students come to a course with a certain level of fear of taking it. Students may interpret the teacher's behavior as being unfair or unsupportive of their learning, resulting in a certain degree of mistrust. ▶ Negative emotional reactions such as fear, or lack of trust in the teacher, can undermine motivation and interfere with learning.
Insufficient prior knowledge	▶ Students vary in how much they know about course content at the start of the course. ▶ Some students may have little to no knowledge about the content, putting them at a disadvantage compared to students with a strong background.
Misconceptions	▶ Students often hold faulty or mistaken beliefs about the course content at the start of the course. ▶ Students may cling to misconceptions even when taught accurate information.

(Continued)

(Continued)

CHALLENGE	DESCRIPTION
Ineffective learning strategies	▶ Students can employ various methods to learn course concepts, and these methods vary widely in effectiveness and efficiency. ▶ Students often prefer the least effective learning strategies.
Transfer of learning	▶ Students can vary in their ability and propensity to apply course concepts appropriately outside the classroom context. ▶ Students often fail to apply knowledge beyond the end of a course.
Constraints of selective attention	▶ Students can focus their awareness on only a limited portion of the environment, missing anything outside that focus. ▶ People mistakenly believe they can multitask, switching attention back and forth among different tasks.
Constraints of mental effort and working memory	▶ Students have two major limitations in cognitive processing, the amount of mental effort or concentration available to them and the ability to hold information consciously. ▶ Students are easily overwhelmed by trying to concentrate on too complex a task or to remember too much information.

Source: Chew and Cerbin (2020).

For example, let's say a student has limited prior knowledge. It doesn't matter the reason that the student lacks this information. This lack of information will interfere with learning because we know that prior knowledge is a predictor of learning. When we build and activate prior knowledge, students learn more. The effect size of using strategies to integrate prior knowledge is 0.93, suggesting a high potential for accelerating learning. Thus, when teachers notice that prior knowledge is missing, they should be encouraged to do something about it. Given the skills that we have collectively developed with interactive videos, students could be introduced to critical information asynchronously. Or the teacher may decide that it's worth the time to have students read some introductory material to build knowledge or provide an overview of the context before beginning the lesson.

> *When we build and activate prior knowledge,*
> *students learn more.*

We have started a list of ways to address these cognitive challenges, based on the recommendations found in the research review by Chew and Cerbin (2020) and the Visible Learning research:

1. **Student mental mindset**: Explain the value and importance of the learning, increase students' ownership of their learning, and explore the habits of minds and mindsets.

2. **Metacognition and self-regulation**: Create reflection assignments, teach students about planning, monitoring, and adjusting their learning, and use practice tests.

3. **Student fear and mistrust**: Focus on teacher credibility, restructure feedback, and create a safe climate for learning and making mistakes.

4. **Insufficient prior knowledge**: Use initial assessments, provide lesson background knowledge and key vocabulary in advance, and use interactive videos.

5. **Misconceptions**: Use advance organizers, recognize common misconceptions for students at a specific age or in a specific content area, and invite students to justify their responses to that thinking.

6. **Ineffective learning strategies**: Teach study skills, model effective strategies with think-alouds, and use spaced practice.

7. **Transfer of learning**: Plan appropriate tasks, model application in different contexts, and tailor feedback to include processing of the task.

8. **Constraints of selective attention**: Increase teacher clarity, use breaks and reorientation strategies, and teach students to avoid multi-tasking, especially with media.

9. **Constraints of mental effort and working memory**: Organize information and chunk it, use both visual and auditory cues (dual coding), and use retrieval practice.

If tutors are able to address the cognitive challenges that confront us all in our learning, imagine how much more students will be able to do. This could be a major accelerator of learning and reduce the deficit thinking that has plagued education for decades.

Conclusion

Tutoring is more complex than many people think. You don't just sit down with a student and tell them information. Many students receiving tutoring services have an internal dialogue that works against them. They might lack confidence or have any number of cognitive barriers to learning. Given that tutors work with individuals or small groups, there is the possibility of recognizing these challenges and helping students work through them. And, if the tutoring is highly effective, students work through these issues and the classroom instruction that they receive will have an even greater impact. To be effective, tutors need to recognize that part of their role is to provide social and emotional support, not just academic support.

Leveraging Relevance and Setting Goals

We are a goal-driven species. Although we may not be consciously aware of it, we establish and complete a number of goals each day. Goals govern our daily living, such as setting an alarm to start the day. We create to-do lists for ourselves to complete errands, and we schedule times to follow up on longer-term professional or personal issues. Some of our goal setting is more overt as we make resolutions about fitness, sleep, or other forms of self-improvement. The assumption that underlies all this goal setting is the belief that we can successfully achieve these goals. Our sense of agency—the belief that we can take action—is the catalyst.

It all seems pretty straightforward—that is, until we encounter students who don't seem to follow through, who can't manage to plan ahead, or who have goals that are vague at best ("I want to get better grades"). Students receiving tutoring support are particularly vulnerable to a lack of agency when it comes to their learning. And that lack of agency makes it especially difficult for them to be able to set goals.

> *Students receiving tutoring support are particularly vulnerable to a lack of agency when it comes to their learning.*

But let's take another look at the examples of goals we set forth in our own adult lives. Whether they are logistical, professional, or related to health and fitness, they each possess an element of personal relevance. We see them as being meaningful in our lives and therefore we make a plan of action to achieve them. And that relevance differs among us as individuals. One person may have a goal of running a marathon, while someone else wants to learn to speak a new language. The relevance of the goal for the individual is an important driver. Students are no different. They benefit from understanding the relevance of what they are learning and why they are learning it.

This chapter addresses two dimensions that can accelerate students' learning. The development of relevance and goals in learning can ignite students and foster a desire in them to invest in themselves. Student ownership of learning is vital, and relevance and goal setting are key.

> *Student ownership of learning is vital, and relevance*
> *and goal setting are key.*

Relevance in Learning

The evidence on relevance as a factor in propelling learning is extensive. Motivation and goal-setting theories name relevancy as a lever for getting students more involved in their learning (Eccles, 2009; Guthrie, et al., 2007). Without question, relevance is in the eye of the beholder. As teachers, we're at a bit of a disadvantage when it comes to determining relevance for our students. We may be older than our students by a decade or more, have different lived experiences, and differ from some of them through a variety of identities, including gender, race, culture, socioeconomic status, and family arrangements. This is not to say that matching students with any of these variables automatically means that we can gauge relevance without their assistance. Instead, it is a reminder of the limitations each of us has when it comes to determining relevance.

Interests range from momentary attention to a deeply valued and self-sustaining investment in becoming more expert about a subject. No group of students is going to uniformly possess identical interest or investment in any topic. The students you are tutoring in a subject are going to possess different interests. One way to consider the range of relevance is across a continuum from least to most relevant (Priniski et al., 2018):

▶ **Personal association** is through a connection to a recalled event, such as learning about the desert because the student's grandparents live in a desert community. Personal association is the least meaningful on the relevance continuum.

▶ **Personal usefulness** extends from a student's belief that this content will help them reach a personal goal. As one example of personal usefulness, a student watches skateboarding videos to learn how to do a new trick.

▶ **Personal identification** is the most motivating type of relevancy and is derived from a deep connection to the content because it resonates with one's identity. For example, a student who describes themselves as a spoken word poet studies both classical poetry and hip-hop lyrics to become more knowledgeable and skilled.

These categories aren't mutually exclusive of one another, and even those that begin as a personal association can blossom into personal identification. The student who was initially interested in deserts because of her grandparents' location can move into personal usefulness as she learns more. She might even set a goal of locating a variety of flora and fauna on her next visit to see them. Relevancy can operate in the other direction as well. The kindergartener who aspires to drive trucks like his stepdad may begin the year wanting to know everything about transportation, only to switch interests and now wanting to know everything about wastewater management because he got interested in a plumbing project at his apartment building.

> *It is useful to probe students' interests at various points throughout the year, not just during the first week of tutoring.*

Interest is not static. It is situational and multidimensional across several constructs from low to high. Issues such as its value, frequency, and mastery shift over time, as virtually any teacher can attest. Topics that a student found absorbing at the beginning of the year may suddenly become boring, while a new interest may replace it. Therefore, it is useful to probe students' interests at various points throughout the year, not just during the first week of tutoring.

Interest is a key lever for building relevancy into learning, as students with a higher degree of interest in a topic are more likely to perform at higher levels (Palmer et al., 2016). Having said that, "interest" isn't likely to manifest itself as a purely academic pursuit. We can't imagine a student breathlessly saying, "I can't wait to learn about the failed Gunpowder Plot of 1604!" But they may be interested in social change, and protests may be a hook for them. They might even be interested in knowing about Guy Fawkes, the leader of the Gunpowder Plot, and the mask that is often worn to disguise the identity of contemporary protesters.

Tutor Gemma Riley meets with seventh grader Kennedy to support her reading. Ms. Riley regularly checks in with her students to learn about their interests so that she can select reading materials that align. Kennedy had told her last week about a program she watched with her mom on alien abductions. "They said that there's this thing called sleep paralysis and that people think something is happening to them, but it really isn't. But I didn't really understand it," said the girl. Ms. Riley found an article written for children on the phenomenon on the website Curious Kids, a feature of the news nonprofit The Conversation (Eckert, 2019). Kennedy not only read and discussed what she learned about sleep paralysis with the tutor, she also chose to write a summary about it as part of her exit ticket. "I learned something, too," said Ms. Riley. "I like pulling in some of their interests to spark up my tutoring sessions."

Use Teacher Clarity to Build Relevance

An advantage we do possess when it comes to establishing relevancy is our knowledge of the content. Why do you need to know about how gases interact? *It helps you better understand what happens each time you take a breath.* Why do you need to know about legends on maps? *It helps you interpret where you are and where you are going when you plan a trip.* Why do you need to know about exponential growth in algebra? *All those COVID-19 pandemic charts have reminded us of the relevance of this concept.*

However, in the rush to make efficient use of tutoring session time, it's easy to overlook establishing the relevancy of the learning to come. It is helpful to keep in mind the three questions that learners of any age have, often unvoiced:

1. What am I learning today?

2. Why am I learning this?

3. How will I know I am successful?

The answers to these three questions lie in teacher clarity, an umbrella term that encompasses three assumptions about learning:

▶ The tutor knows what students are supposed to be learning.

▶ The students know what they are supposed to be learning.

▶ The tutor and students know what success looks like.

Taken together, these three aspects contribute to teacher clarity, which has an effect size of 0.75. Fendick (1990) defined teacher clarity as "a measure of the clarity of communication between teachers and students in both directions" (p. 10). This two-way communication is further supported through the use of learning intentions and success criteria. Learning intentions give students a clear idea of the purpose of the lesson:

▸ *I am learning about gas exchange in the cardiopulmonary system.*

▸ *I am learning about the map legends used to show location and direction.*

▸ *I am learning about the properties of exponential functions.*

Students should also know what success will look like for them, as it aids them in applying what they have been learning. Success criteria are a positive influence on learning, with an effect size of 0.88:

▸ *I can accurately sequence the process of gas exchange in the cardiopulmonary system.*

▸ *I can use the legends on the school map to describe the walk from my classroom to the playground.*

▸ *I can explain the properties of a graphed exponential function.*

Now add a statement of relevancy that addresses the question "Why am I learning this?" Keep in mind that relevancy may extend from personal association to personal identity and is likely to be varied among students.

▸ *The gas exchange in the cardiopulmonary system explains what occurs when a person hyperventilates and why deep breathing assists when this happens.*

▸ *Reading a map correctly helps me get to other places without getting lost!*

▸ *Exponential functions are used by epidemiologists to model the spread of COVID-19 under various conditions.*

Some tutors display the word "Why?" prominently in their workspace as a reminder to students that if relevance hasn't been established, they should ask about it. Others write a relevance statement so that the student and the tutor can refer to it during the lesson. In addition, you can augment these with tailored relevance statements for individuals. Telling a student "I know you want to be an EMT, and managing a patient's breathing is something you'll be doing as part of emergency treatment" signals to the student your knowledge about their aspirations and how you see the relevancy of what they'll be learning in a more personal way.

Embedded within learning intentions, success criteria and relevance statements are the effect they have on the learner. They can cause the student to plan and predict, set goals, and acquire a stronger sense of how to judge their own progress. These procedures allow for discussion and negotiation with the student about what constitutes mastery, rather than leaving such understanding to chance.

Goal Setting in Learning

Students receiving tutoring often require assistance in setting goals. These goals can be academic goals for the completion of course work but can be further strengthened by imbuing them with *agency* or the recognition that there is a relationship between effort and outcomes. For example, a goal to "Ace my homework" is not especially useful—it is vague, doesn't have a time limit, lacks details in terms of the student tracking their progress, and, worst of all in terms of agency, doesn't have any kind of action plan to go with it. Solid goals meet four conditions (Martin, 2006). They are

▶ Specific in nature

▶ Challenging to the student

▶ Competitively self-referenced

▶ Based on self-improvement

These are goals set by the student, not by someone else.

We are fans of a personal-best approach to goal setting (Martin, 2006). These growth-oriented goals are set by the student to improve on previous performance. An important element shouldn't be lost—these are goals set by the student, not by someone else. They can be outcome goals, such as "Improve my comprehension skills so I can achieve a new benchmark in my reading level," or process oriented, such as reading for fifteen minutes every evening. Notice that neither of these goals involves comparisons to others; they have mastery, rather than performance, in mind. Because the goal is co-constructed with the student, personal-best goals are associated with higher levels of intrinsic motivation, persistence, engagement, and enjoyment of school (Martin, 2011). Goals set with students can be personal ("Try out for the gymnastics team") or nonacademic but school related (attendance).

Tutors can strengthen students' personal link to the goal by discussing why it is of value to them. Too often young people will go through a goal-setting exercise because an adult is insisting on it. When you talk with them about why the goal is important to them (not to their school, family, or friends), you further foster their sense of agency about the decisions they make and the direction they choose. Don't get discouraged if their initial goals don't seem all that substantial. You are building a habit and a disposition for them. Regaining one's agency takes time and it also takes early and small wins.

> *Students will never know how you have used your agency if all they see are the outcomes, not the path you took to get there.*

Importantly, it isn't so much the initial goal setting that has an effect, but rather what is done with it. If a goal is set but never revisited, it holds little to no value. Check in regularly with students to discuss their progress and adjust their planned actions as needed. Knowing that their plans can be adjusted based on new circumstances can be an eye-opener for students. They often look at the adults in their lives and see the accomplishments, but not all the zigzags it took to get there. These conferences are a great time to share your story and struggles and, in the process, build a relationship. And keep in mind that there is incredible value in seeing agency modeled. But students will never know how you have used your agency if all they see are the outcomes, not the path you took to get there. An example of a personal goal-setting tool is in Figure 3.1.

Figure 3.1   Planning Tool for a Personal-Best Goal-Setting Conference

What is an academic, school-related, or personal goal you have for yourself?

> ❯ Why is this something you value?
>
> ❯ What has your past performance been like? What has been your personal best so far?
>
> ❯ How will achieving this goal benefit you?
>
> ❯ How will you know you have been successful?
>
> ❯ What might get in the way of you meeting this goal?
>
> ❯ What do you need to achieve this goal?

RESOURCES	SELF	SCHOOL	FAMILY

Action steps to achieve this goal:

1.

2.

3.

We will check in with each other every _____ weeks to talk about your progress toward your personal-best goal.

Goal Orientation

When you strive for challenge, you establish personal goals, and not just any goals: your goal orientation is important. As discussed in the introduction, goal orientation can be either mastery or performance. Martin (2013) explains, "Mastery orientation is focused on factors and processes such as effort, self-improvement, skill development, learning, and the task at hand. Performance orientation is focused more on demonstrating relative ability, social comparison, and outperforming others" (p. 353). In other words, it's the difference between saying "I want to learn to speak Spanish" (mastery) and "I want to get an A in Spanish" (performance).

A second dimension of goal orientation is approach versus avoidance. *Approach goals* are directed toward obtaining something positive, while *avoidance goals* are about actions that are intended to avoid a negative outcome. There's a subtle but important difference between "I want to get an A in Spanish" and "I don't want to flunk Spanish." Emotions underlie each of these, and avoidance goals are sometimes fueled by a desire, above all else, not to expose one's lack of knowledge or skills for fear of being judged. Approach and avoidance orientations intersect with mastery and performance goals (see Figure 3.2).

Figure 3.2 Goal Orientations

	MASTERY	PERFORMANCE
Approach	Strive to learn a task	Do better than before (improvement)
Avoidance	Not interested in trying to avoid looking incompetent	Avoid doing worse than before (maintain)

Listen carefully for students who express an avoidance orientation, likely to be more common among those who are being tutored. An avoidance orientation, be they mastery or performance goals, is not going to deliver breakthrough results. Tutor Isiah Morales heard this when Nicholás, a tenth-grade student, told him his math goal was to "drop this algebra class. It's too hard, I failed it before, and I don't even see the point." Nicholás went on to explain that "this tutoring thing is a waste of time."

> *Listen carefully for students who express an avoidance orientation.*

Mr. Morales understood that there was quite a bit of negative emotion behind the student's beliefs and that a single conversation was not going to change Nicholás's mind. "I'll tell you what," said the tutor, "let's just take one week at a time. How about if we review what you're learning in class this week, and we'll just focus on that? Let's break down what it is you know first."

The tutor suspects that Nicholás is experiencing several challenges brought on by his thinking, including a mental mindset and constraints of mental effort (see Chapter 2). Later Mr. Morales said, "It's going to take some time with him. Right now, I want to get some early wins for him to restore some confidence in his ability."

Use Their Goals to Highlight Successes

Do you know that feeling when you are trying to make your way through a dark and unfamiliar room? Your senses are heightened as you strain to see and hear, hoping for a clue. You move slowly and cautiously for fear you'll run into something or even fall. But switch the light on, and you visibly relax as you move with more assurance. Student self-reflection works like a light—it illuminates a path that makes acceleration possible.

Students need opportunities to regularly reflect on their progress. This builds their confidence, allows them to make plans for improvement, and reinforces their awareness of their skills (a metacognitive trait). Further, these should happen through the learning process.

At the beginning of a set of tutoring sessions, share the success criteria with the student and allow them to rank-order the relative level of difficulty for each item. Although this is in advance of instruction, it provides the student with an opportunity to consider their present skill level and to make early decisions about where they will need to concentrate more effort. The feedback to you is quite helpful, too. Imagine knowing at the start of a unit who already is feeling as though they may have more difficulty than you anticipated. This presents opportunities to provide instruction on gaps in skills or concepts, as well as to provide students with feedback about their agency. Figure 3.3 presents an example from a fifth-grade math unit on multiplying multi-digit whole numbers. Notice how this particular student said that using math strategies flexibly would probably be the most difficult.

Figure 3.3 Self-Ranking of Success Criteria

Difficulty	Success Criteria for Unit
How difficult will this be for you? (1 = easy, 2 = challenging, 3 = more challenging, 4 = difficult)	I can multiply multi-digit whole numbers in real-world problem-solving situations.
3	I can demonstrate my understanding of an algorithm of a single-digit factor.
4	I can use math strategies flexibly.
1	I can recognize math terms (multiply, product, algorithm).
2	I can use a standard algorithm.

A second technique for prompting self-reflection about progress is to compare assessments over a period. This type of assessment, called ipsative assessment, is used to compare a student's past performance to a current one (Isaacs et al., 2013). Teachers often do ipsative evaluation to gauge growth over time, but it is less common for students to do so. This process allows the student to notice where growth has occurred and is self-referential (*how did I do compared to 6 weeks ago?*) rather than peer-oriented (*how did I do compared to my classmates?*). You see young children delight in doing this when they compare a drawing they did at age 3 to another they made at age 6. These comparative self-assessments can be especially motivating for learners who have larger attainment gaps compared to the grade-level expectations, as it allows them to view their growth and developmental progress (Hughes et al., 2014). Figure 3.4 is an example of an ipsative assessment about writing. The student compares two pieces of writing, one from earlier in the semester and a more recent one, to identify where they have grown and where to focus effort.

Figure 3.4   Comparative Self-Assessment for Informational Writing in Grade 6

Title and Date of First Essay	Title and Date of Second Essay
ORGANIZATION/PURPOSE	
Topic is introduced clearly to preview what is to follow 4 3 2 1	Topic is introduced clearly to preview what is to follow 4 3 2 1
Ideas and concepts are organized using definition, classification, or compare/contrast 4 3 2 1	Ideas and concepts are organized using definition, classification, or compare/contrast 4 3 2 1
Transitions create cohesion and show relationships among ideas 4 3 2 1	Transitions create cohesion and show relationships among ideas 4 3 2 1
A concluding statement supports the explanation given 4 3 2 1	A concluding statement supports the explanation given 4 3 2 1
Task, purpose, and audience are aligned to prompt 4 3 2 1	Task, purpose, and audience are aligned to prompt 4 3 2 1
EVIDENCE/ELABORATION	
Develops the topic with relevant facts, definitions, details, and examples 4 3 2 1	Develops the topic with relevant facts, definitions, details, and examples 4 3 2 1
Follows a standard format for citations 4 3 2 1	Follows a standard format for citations 4 3 2 1

EVIDENCE/ELABORATION	
Skillfully quotes and paraphrases 4 3 2 1	Skillfully quotes and paraphrases 4 3 2 1
Uses relevant information from multiple sources 4 3 2 1	Uses relevant information from multiple sources 4 3 2 1
Effective and appropriate style enhances content 4 3 2 1	Effective and appropriate style enhances content 4 3 2 1
CONVENTIONS	
Demonstrates grade-level grammar, usage, and conventions 4 3 2 1	Demonstrates grade-level grammar, usage, and conventions 4 3 2 1

Source: Fisher et al. (2021).

Conclusion

Students in tutoring are often uncertain about their learning. In addition, they may be unsure of whether there is even any purpose to their learning. Building relevance into tutoring sessions allows students to see themselves in the lessons. In addition, relevance can boost their confidence because they can appreciate how much they already know about a topic. A fundamental principle is that learning happens when we attach new knowledge to existing knowledge. Relevance allows you as the tutor to move from the known to the new. Couple this approach with goal setting to encourage students to own their learning—as with relevance, there is a big payoff. Goals make it possible for you to draw students' attention to their incremental successes. Nothing motivates like success, and short-term goals let them experience success early and often.

Learning to Learn

"I read this chapter, but I don't get it," laments eighth grader Jamila. "Can you help me?" Tutors are regularly asked this question and there's a good deal of hopefulness on the part of the student. Maybe, they think, you'll be able to explain it all to them and they'll *finally* understand. They just need to listen more carefully, right?

Well, no. Too often students possess a naive belief that learning is about cramming as much stuff in your head as possible. The people who do the best, they reason, are those who can memorize an extraordinary amount of information. It's a party trick, rather than a set of habits and dispositions. Without intending to, we contribute to this false belief by using what Paul (1995) calls "mother robin teaching": we chew up information for them and feed it into the baby bird's beak. The result, he notes, is that students incorrectly believe the following:

> "I can't understand anything unless you tell me exactly what to say and think. I need you to figure out everything for me. I shouldn't have to do more than repeat what you or the textbook says."

The solution, Paul goes on to say, is to foster a disposition of "figuring things out for yourself."

> *Some students need to be taught* how to learn.

This is not to say that tough love is the way to go—"Good luck with that!" is not the proper message. Rather, it means that some students need to be taught *how to learn*. The goal of tutoring is to create independent learners, not tutor-dependent learners. In this chapter, we'll discuss the role of struggle in learning, then shift to ways to infuse learning strategies into instruction through the use of study skills.

The Case for Struggle in Learning

Let's get real. No one likes to be wrong. When was the last time you failed at doing something and cheerily reminded yourself, "Now I've got an opportunity to learn!" The failure to accomplish something can be demoralizing, especially in the absence of support. However, failure can also be productive, especially when it is followed by further learning and feedback. Imagine if schools were places where errors were celebrated as opportunities to learn. Over time, we might all learn to welcome the opportunities that our errors provide us for learning. The core premise of Dweck's (2006) powerful work on fostering a growth mindset is predicated on regular encounters with struggle.

> *Imagine if schools were places where errors were celebrated as opportunities to learn.*

However, keep in mind that failure can be unproductive, and so can success. The context of the failure or success is crucial. Kapur (2016) describes four possible learning events:

▶ **Unproductive failure** (unguided problem solving)

▶ **Unproductive success** (memorizing an algorithm without understanding why)

▶ **Productive failure** (using prior knowledge to figure out a solution, followed by more instruction)

▶ **Productive success** (structured problem solving)

Of the four conditions, unproductive failure yields the smallest gains, as the thinking is not guided in any way, and people are just expected to discover what should be learned. Unproductive success is also of limited value, as individuals in this condition rely on memorization only but don't ever get to why and how this is applied (think of the baby bird that has everything intellectually chewed up for it). There's just no transfer of knowledge.

Now let's move to the beneficial conditions: productive failure and productive success. Kapur explains that

The difference between productive failure and productive success is a subtle but an important one. The goal for productive failure is a preparation for learning from subsequent instruction. Thus, it does not matter if students do not achieve successful problem-solving performance initially. In contrast, the goal for productive success is to learn through a successful problem-solving activity itself. (p. 293)

Based on Kapur's model, we identified four possible learning events and their impact (see Figure 4.1). Effective tutoring requires a mixture of productive failure and productive success. We use productive failure as a means to expose a problem the student didn't know existed, and then to follow it with instruction. Kapur suggests that "the first job of a teacher isn't to teach. The first job of a teacher is to prepare your students to see and then to show them" (2019).

"The first job of a teacher isn't to teach.
The first job of a teacher is to prepare your students
to see and then to show them."

An added benefit of having some productive failure events is that they activate the student's prior knowledge. As we have stated previously, new knowledge is built on a foundation of prior knowledge. However, if that prior knowledge just lies there, it's useless. It's like having a great tool in your garage that doesn't get used because you forgot it was there. Tutor Luis Ortega watches his fourth-grade math students solve a fun challenge question at the beginning of the session so that he can watch how they use their prior knowledge and reasoning. One morning he asked Julia, "Would you rather have 33 quarters or 173 nickels?" He then listened to her reasoning and observed her problem-solving skills. Although it seemed like a straightforward calculation problem, she had difficulty in setting up the problem. "It was the perfect opportunity to do some instruction on properties of operations, and to explain her reasoning," said Mr. Ortega. Most importantly, the experience gave Mr. Ortega a chance to talk about struggle and persistence.

"Her tolerance for not immediately having the answer is getting better," he said. "She's beginning to see that she has the stamina to stick with a problem and not immediately give up and say it's too hard."

Figure 4.1 Four Possible Learning Events

	UNPRODUCTIVE FAILURE	UNPRODUCTIVE SUCCESS	PRODUCTIVE SUCCESS	PRODUCTIVE FAILURE
Type of learning event	Unguided problem solving without further instruction	Rote memorization without conceptual understanding	Guided problem solving using prior knowledge and tasks planned for success	Unsuccessful or suboptimal problem-solving using prior knowledge, followed by further instruction
Learning outcome	Frustration that leads to abandoning learning	Completion of the task without understanding its purpose or relevance	Consolidation of learning through scaffolded practice	Learning from errors that ensures learners persist in generating and exploring representations and solutions
Useful for			Surface learning of new knowledge firmly anchored to prior knowledge	Deep learning and transfer of knowledge
Undermines	Agency and motivation	Goal setting and willingness to seek challenge		
Promotes			Skill development and concept attainment	Use of cognitive, metacognitive, and affective strategies

Source: Frey et al. (2018).

Study Skills and Learning

Effective studying involves three dimensions: cognitive, metacognitive, and affective. All three of these are important and together impact learning. Study skills are an above-average tool for ensuring students learn with an effect size of 0.45. Having said that, many students use ineffective study techniques that fail to yield expected results. When they don't work, students abandon the idea of studying altogether. For older students, in particular, this triggers a downward slide. They cling to the idea that seat time in class should be enough. In doing so, they fail to develop the habits and dispositions of studying.

What Doesn't Work

Cramming, also known as massed practice, runs counter to the idea of studying. In massed practice, tasks are completed in periods that are close together. Often, the information is lost if not rehearsed thereafter. Who hasn't attempted to "study" all night for a test, only to forget everything? Conversely, spaced practice is distributed and rehearsed over longer periods, resulting in sustained retention. This has direct implications for teachers as they assign tasks for students to complete. If we want students to learn, and to engage in study skills as a pathway for learning, then we have to ensure that they have opportunities for spaced practice.

Studying is a habit that is useful beyond the preK–12 system and is especially powerful as students transition into college and career settings. Individuals without strong study skills are less likely to be successful and are more likely to be dependent on others. Thankfully, we can change that. We can teach students to leverage the right tools for studying.

> *We can teach students to leverage*
> *the right tools for studying.*

Cognitive Study Skills

There are many tools students can learn and use to study. We advocate teaching students a range of cognitive study skills and then giving them opportunities to choose skills to use. Many of these cognitive skills are for initial surface learning of skills and concepts.

Read With a Pencil

The notes in a book can reveal much about the reader. Edgar Allan Poe, himself an unapologetic penciler, wrote "in the marginalia, too, we talk only to ourselves; we therefore talk freshly—boldly—originally—with abandonment—without conceit" (1844, ¶ 4). The practice of making notes to oneself during reading was a widespread practice for centuries but fell out of favor in the twentieth century as public libraries became common. To write in a book was thought to sully it somehow. To be sure, writing in a text that doesn't belong to you isn't looked upon kindly. But in the process of protecting the public books, we forgot about the gains to be had from writing in one that belongs to us alone. In their seminal text *How to Read a Book*, Adler and Van Doren (1972) laid out a case for engaging in repeated readings with accompanying annotation:

> Why is marking a book indispensable to reading it? First, it keeps you awake—not merely conscious, but wide awake. Second, reading, if active, is thinking, and thinking tends to express itself in words, spoken or written. The person who says he knows what he thinks but cannot express it usually does not know what he thinks. Third, writing your reactions down helps you remember the thoughts of the author. (p. 49)

Keep annotation simple for students. The most common annotation marks we use:

▸ **Underline** major points.

▸ **Circle** keywords or phrases that are confusing or unknown to you.

▸ Use a **question mark (?)** for questions that you have during the reading. Be sure to write your question.

When Marc Bellinger, Jamila's tutor, heard her say, "I read this chapter, but I don't get it," he asked her to select a passage she was having trouble with, and they annotated it together.

"She's a reasonably good reader," he said, "but she has a naive understanding of her ability to hold extensive amounts of information in her mind. Some of my students think that reading is reading, whether it's a novel you're reading at the beach or an explanation about a complicated science phenomenon."

Mr. Bellinger didn't review the entire chapter with her. Instead, he made a plan for finishing the rest of the reading on her own using the annotation process.

"She's been taught this before, but she hasn't really internalized it as a process she can use on her own. Part of what I can do is to remind her about what she knows and guide her about how to use these learning skills."

Use Notes, Don't Just Take Notes

Taking notes isn't really a study skill, but studying the notes can help students learn. Unfortunately, some students never look at their notes after taking them. And sometimes, we ruin opportunities to study. For example, split page notes, such as the Cornell format, are useful for studying when students take the notes in the major column and then later, after the information has been recorded, reread their notes and identify the significant topics and record them in the minor column and then summarize each page. They can then cover the notes and read the significant topics and see what they remember.

There is perhaps no more widely taught note-taking system than Cornell notes. Cornell Reading and Study Center director Walter Pauk developed this method in the 1950s as a means for law students to study for bar exams. He taught students how to divide their note pages into three sections (see Figure 4.2), giving them space to describe the details covered in a lecture, with the other sections left for after the lecture is over. Writing the notes is just the first step; Pauk's system stresses the importance of how the notes are used after the lecture, using a method some have called "the six R's" (Pauk & Owens, 2010):

- ▶ **Record** the lecture notes in the main section of the note page.

- ▶ **Reduce** the essential ideas by reviewing the notes within 24 hours and phrasing these ideas as questions.

- ▶ **Recite** the information aloud by answering these questions while keeping the notes portion covered.

- ▶ **Reflect** by asking oneself about how well the material is understood, and what clarifying questions should be asked of the teacher.

- ▶ **Review** during subsequent short study sessions.

- ▶ **Recapitulate** the main ideas by writing them in the Summary section.

Figure 4.2   Cornell Notes Template

CUES	NOTES
Use this area for main ideas.	Record lecture notes here during class. Use meaningful abbreviations and symbols. Leave space to add additional information.
Phrase cues as questions.	
Fill this in within 24 hours after class.	

SUMMARY
Main ideas and major points are recorded here. These are written during later review sessions.

Many middle and high school programs teach students Cornell note-taking. The high school where tutor Samara Abaza works does so, and she makes the most of it. A portion of one session each week is dedicated to teaching and practicing study skills. Her students bring the Cornell notes they have developed in their classes, and she focuses their attention on how they are reducing, reciting, and reflecting on the material. "Sometimes it's just working through a few pages of notes," said Ms. Abaza. "Then we set a study goal together. I keep the dialogue going about studying. I tell them that they need to help me help them."

Metacognitive Study Skills

Teaching students how to think about their thinking is a valuable study skill. Simply put, students should be aware of the *when, why,* and *how* components of what they are learning. An important distinction is that metacognition is not reflection. Instead, metacognitive skills require active self-monitoring processes that occur during the act of learning, not as a reflective afterthought. An effective metacognitive method is to teach students to intentionally consider both the advantages and disadvantages of a given function within the learning context. *What are the benefits of renewable energy? Are there drawbacks to this approach? What will happen if we continue using fossil fuels as the alternative? How do these pros/cons affect me?* This helpful questioning approach allows students to become facilitators of their own learning, giving them a powerful organizational tool for processing complex information and concepts.

The following strategies can help you develop students' metacognitive study skills.

Goal Setting

Invite students to create mastery goals rather than performance goals. You'll recall that performance goals ("I will get an A on the test") are not bad, but they don't direct the studying students need to do. Rather, when students set goals such as "I can solve linear equations" or "I can say the names of the planets in order" or "I can summarize the events leading up to World War I," students focus on gaps in their learning and then attempt to close those gaps.

Planning

In addition to any time allocated for students to study, metacognitive study skills require that students plan their studying. It's helpful to introduce study skills so that you can monitor students and provide feedback, but this needs to be transferred to home. At first, students can identify times for studying and what they will study. When they have evidence of what they need to practice, their planning is typically more productive.

Monitoring and Self-Assessment

Students need tools to develop the habit of monitoring their studying. Self-assessment tools can be used by the student to monitor their changes in understanding. In addition, students can learn to monitor their time on task when studying. You'll recall that interrupted attention is a cognitive barrier, as some students believe incorrectly that they can multitask. Monitoring cognitive engagement is a metacognitive skill that we can develop. Students sometimes have difficulty getting started in their studying. Third-grade tutor Regan Carter uses a checklist when her students are in the classroom or at home and find themselves stuck (see Figure 4.3). "I have them glue this to the inside cover of their notebook so they can look at it and self-assess to figure out what should happen next."

Figure 4.3   What to Do When You Don't Know What to Do

I CAN'T GET STARTED IN MY LEARNING	
What can I do on my own?	▶ I can reread the directions to make sure I didn't miss something. ▶ I can review the success criteria. ▶ I can use any resources given to me for help.
What can I do with a peer?	▶ I can ask my peer to explain what we should be doing. ▶ I can share the question I have with a peer to see if they could help. ▶ I can ask my peer to show me how they got started.

I CAN'T GET STARTED IN MY LEARNING	
What can I do with the teacher?	▸ I can make sure I understand what I am supposed to be doing.
	▸ I can walk through an example with the teacher.
	▸ I can ask the teacher to support me in getting started.

Source: Fisher et al. (2019a).

Reflecting

Following a study session, students should reflect on the experience. They should learn to spend a few minutes thinking about what they just did and analyze their efforts. Reflection questions can be used to facilitate this habit. Consider the following questions and their potential to encourage reflection:

Did I remain focused during the study period?

Did I accomplish my goals for this session?

What do I understand now that I didn't understand before?

What am I ready to teach someone else?

Ninth-grade math tutor Rick Hansen encourages his students to reflect at the end of their math homework to facilitate their ability to see their own progress (see Figure 4.4). "They can get pretty overwhelmed. I want to make sure they are conscious of their progress and that they know where the gaps are," he said.

Cognitive and metacognitive study skills are important and are likely to improve students' learning. As students experience success with studying, their affective skills are also impacted. Students with strong affective skills study more often and begin to attribute success to their efforts. We all use evidence of impact to decide how to allocate resources. When students see that studying does good things for them, their affective skills grow and they are much more likely to engage in study behaviors in the future.

Figure 4.4 Self-Assess Your Progress

	I'M A PRO AND CAN TEACH OTHERS.	I'M ABLE TO DO THIS ON MY OWN.	I'M STILL PRACTICING BUT ALMOST THERE.	I NEED MORE HELP.
Directions: Capture the success criteria for the learning intention provided by your teacher in the boxes below. Prior to the end of the lesson, self-assess your progress by determining your performance level for each success criterion below.				
SUCCESS CRITERIA 1:				
Evidence to support current performance level:				
My next learning steps:				
SUCCESS CRITERIA 2:				
Evidence to support current performance level:				
My next learning steps:				

Source: Fisher et al. (2019b).

Affective Study Skills

These are the moods, feelings, and beliefs that students have. In this case, we're talking about their beliefs about studying. Students with strong affective study skills are motivated and define themselves as students, or those who study.

Motivation

Success is motivating. Students need some early wins in which they see the impact of their studying on their performance. Extrinsic rewards, such as stickers for studying for ten minutes or ten points to complete the review guide, do not motivate students to study on their own, and they do not ensure that students' affective states are changed. Rather, motivation develops when students see the return on investment. Let them have a few early wins and show them that their efforts paid off. Over time, motivation will grow, especially when mastery goals are involved.

Mood

Mood is a powerful motivator. We can't control the mood of our students, as there are many outside influences, but we can help students set the mood before they study. When they take action to focus on their mood, they are more likely to have a beneficial study session.

Self-Concept

The stories students tell about themselves to themselves become their identity. These identities are shaped by the people around them, including their teachers. As adults interact with students, we need to keep their developing identities in mind. What we say, and how we say it, influences students' thinking about themselves and how likely they are to engage in learning tasks such as studying. Be careful and wisely choose words that build students' sense of self.

> *The stories students tell about themselves to themselves become their identity.*

Elementary tutor Gina Colaizzi keeps a poster of the cognitive, metacognitive, and affective study skills her students can apply (see Figure 4.5). "They don't really study formally," she said. "At least, not

Figure 4.5   Learning How to Learn

I can take notes.	I can make a plan for my project.	I can be excited to learn.
I can use a graphic organizer.	I can keep track of my own learning.	I can make sure I am in a good spot to learn.
I can summarize what I read.	I can correct my mistakes.	I can make sure I have enough time for my assignment.
I can make flashcards.	I can make changes to my work.	I can get through a challenge.
I can reread.	I can self-assess my work.	I can set goals.
I can memorize important information.	I can use self-questioning.	I can be ready to solve problems.
I can keep track of my understanding.	I can review vocabulary words to make sure I know what they mean.	I can use my comprehension strategies when I am not sure that I understood what I read.

Source: Fisher et al. (2019a).

yet. But I want to build the habits of learning into their daily practices. Whether they are with me in a session, or in their classroom, or at home, I want them to see how they take ownership of their learning."

Conclusion

Learning is a process of "figuring things out" under the guidance of a caring adult. This requires that students know how to learn. Unfortunately, many believe that learning means regurgitating information. In truth, learning requires that students engage with the content in deeper ways. They need to reflect on what they know and don't know. Processes that are commonly called "study skills" are in truth the habits and dispositions of learning. These are the cognitive, metacognitive, and affective tools they can utilize, if only they are afforded opportunities to do so. A major tutoring trap is in reinforcing the notion that learning is limited to recitation and reproduction. Let's make sure we are building increasingly independent learners.

Learning Content

··

The unrealized learning potential that some students experience manifests itself in content knowledge gaps. Tutoring is an important tool for addressing the complex academic needs of students who don't possess the prior knowledge and habits they need to learn new content. While some of the learning gains that students need to make fall into the category of "learning how to learn," other aspects require more content-specific approaches. There are some fundamental practices that educators use to ensure that learning is occurring. These are augmented by instructional practices that forward students' reading, writing, and mathematics skills. In this chapter, we discuss evidence-based practices that should be featured in every session. Later, we discuss tools for ensuring that students are progressing in the subject matter.

Fundamentals of Teaching

Many of the instructional principles that apply to large group instruction remain the same when tutoring individuals or small groups of students. A given is that assessment forms the bedrock of good teaching. Students in tutoring support have likely been identified because the results of a standards-based assessment have shown that they have not made expected progress. These data may be supplemented with further diagnostic assessments designed to locate more specifically where their difficulties lie.

> *Assessment forms the bedrock of good teaching.*

Tutoring sessions should be framed using a consistent lesson planning template. This allows you to track the progress of students, align instruction to standards, and utilize evidence-based practices from the learning sciences. An added benefit is that it provides you with an organizational system for chronicling your work with individual students. Figure 5.1 is a planning template you can use and customize for your context. We'll discuss most of the dimensions of the

Figure 5.1   Planning Tool Template

Assessed need: I have noticed that my student needs:
Standard(s) addressed:
Text(s) I will use:
Clarity: Learning intention for this lesson:
Clarity: Success criteria for this lesson:
Direct Instruction Model (e.g., think-aloud)—strategies/skills/concepts to emphasize: Guide and scaffold—questions to ask: Assess to check for understanding:
Dialogic Instruction Teacher-directed tools (e.g., anticipation guides, K-W-L) to spark discussion: Assess to check for understanding:
Feedback opportunities:
Independent learning and closure:

Source: Adapted from Fisher et al. (2017).

planning template in this chapter. Remember that we discussed feedback in Chapter 2. In addition, we will address independent learning and practice in Chapter 6.

Teach for Clarity

You'll recall from the discussion in Chapter 3 that clarity is the compilation of organizing instruction, explaining content, providing examples, guided practice, and assessment of learning. These specific components of clarity are rooted in the planning process and make the content and practices accessible to the learners. We communicate clarity to students through learning intentions, success criteria, and explicit connections to why this learning is relevant to them.

Start your sessions with a discussion of these three points. It only takes a few minutes, and the reward is higher levels of cognitive engagement, goal setting, and personal ownership of the learning. A useful frame for capturing each of these is this:

> "I am learning _____ so that _____. I'll know that I know it when _____."

- **Geography:** I am learning <u>where I live in the universe</u> so that <u>I know where I am and where I can go</u>. I'll know that I know it <u>when I can explain exactly where I live by planet, continent, country, state, city, and address</u>.

- **Writing:** I am learning <u>how to write opinion paragraphs</u> so that <u>I can explain my opinions and convince others</u>. I'll know that I know it <u>when a reader can explain my opinion after reading my paragraph</u>.

- **Science:** I am learning <u>about energy in different phases of matter</u> so that <u>I can understand the movement of molecules</u>. I'll know that I know it when <u>I can explain the relationship between pressure, temperatures, and changes in the state of matter</u>.

- **Algebra:** I am learning <u>to graph absolute value functions</u> so that <u>I can determine whether the function opens up or down</u>. I'll know that I know it when <u>I can use the slope to plot the remaining points</u>.

Model Your Thinking

Thinking is invisible. Students often believe that you just "know" something and fail to recognize that you are actually making a number of internal decisions as you use a process or procedure. Modeling, paired with thinking aloud, can trigger student understanding about the cognitive and metacognitive moves needed to complete a task. In doing so, students can learn how to think aloud about their own decision making and problem solving, providing you with further insight into the student's grasp of skills and concepts. Providing examples of thinking is useful, but effective modeling includes an explanation of why teachers are doing what they are doing so that students understand *how* the teacher was able to think, not just *what* the teacher was thinking.

Think-alouds use "I" statements. A lot of adults say "we" or "you" in their explanations, but "I" statements—using the first-person pronoun—do something different and more powerful for the brains of students. They activate the ability—some call it an instinct—of humans to learn by imitation.

> *"I" statements—using the first-person pronoun—*
> *do something different and more powerful*
> *for the brains of students.*

Add the word *because* as you think aloud; it's important to explain *why* you're thinking what you're thinking. If not, students experience an example but do not know how to do this on their own. Using *because* reduces the chance that students will be left wondering how you knew to do something or why you think a certain way. For example, while modeling the comprehension strategy of predicting, you might say, "I can make the following prediction [insert the prediction] because the author told me . . . ." Or you might say, "I can visualize this in my mind because of these three words."

Including the *why* while modeling increases the chance that the student will be able to imitate the expert thinking they have witnessed, because they are provided with examples and the reasons for those examples. Thinking about your thinking is a metacognitive act, and students will start to think more metacognitively when they hear others do so.

Guide and Scaffold

This aspect of the learning focuses on guiding student thinking while avoiding the temptation to tell them what to think. This requires that tutors ask the right question to get the student to do the cognitive work and teach the student how to ask powerful questions. Questioning has an effect size of 0.48.

> *When questions fail to ensure success,*
> *tutors can rely on prompts and cues.*

When questions fail to ensure success, tutors can rely on prompts and cues. In general, prompts are statements made by the adult to focus the student on the cognitive and metacognitive processes needed to complete a learning task. Metacognitive strategies have an effect size of 0.55. When teachers provide prompts, they apprentice the student into cognitive and metacognitive thinking. Cues, on the other hand, are designed to shift a student's attention. Sometimes, students need this level of support to work through something confusing. Figures 5.2 and 5.3 have examples of prompts and cues.

Figure 5.2   Types of Prompts

TYPE OF PROMPT	DEFINITION	EXAMPLE
Background knowledge	Reference to content that the student already knows, has been taught, or has experienced but has temporarily forgotten or is not applying correctly.	▶ When trying to solve a right-triangle problem, the tutor says, "What do you recall about the degrees inside a triangle?" ▶ As part of a science passage about the water cycle, the tutor says, "What do you remember about states of matter?" ▶ When reading about a trip to the zoo, the tutor says, "Remember when you had a field trip to the zoo last month? Do you recall how you felt when it started to rain?"

(Continued)

(Continued)

TYPE OF PROMPT	DEFINITION	EXAMPLE
Process or procedure	Reference to established or generally agreed-upon representation, rules, or guidelines that the student is not following due to error or misconception.	▶ When a student incorrectly orders fractions, thinking the greater the denominator, the greater the fraction, the tutor might say, "Draw a picture of each fraction. What do you notice about the size of the fraction and the number in the denominator?" ▶ When a student is unsure about how to start solving a problem, the tutor says, "Think about which of the problem-solving strategies we have used that might help you to get started." ▶ The student is saying a word incorrectly and the tutor says, "When two vowels go walking . . . ." ▶ When the student has difficulty starting to develop a writing outline, the tutor says, "I'm thinking about the mnemonic we've used for organizing an explanatory article."
Reflective	Promotion of metacognition—getting the student to think about their thinking—so that the student can use the resulting insight to determine	▶ The student has just produced a solution incorrectly, and the tutor says, "Does that make sense? Think about the numbers you are working with and the meaning of the operation." ▶ A tutor says, "I see you're thinking strategically. What would be the next logical step?"

TYPE OF PROMPT	DEFINITION	EXAMPLE
	the next steps or the solution to a problem.	▶ When the student fails to include evidence in her writing, the tutor says, "Think about what we're learning today. Can you recall the purpose?"
Heuristic	Engagement in an informal, self-directed problem-solving procedure; the approach the student comes up with does not have to be like anyone else's approach, but it does need to work.	▶ When the student does not get the correct answer to a math problem, the tutor says, "Maybe drawing a visual representation would help you see the problem." ▶ When the student has difficulty explaining the relationships between characters in a text, the tutor says, "Maybe drawing a visual representation of the main character's connections to one another will help you." ▶ When a student gets stuck and cannot think of what to write next, the tutor says, "Writers have a lot of different ways for getting unstuck. Some just write whatever comes to mind, others create a visual, others talk it out with a reader, and others take a break and walk around for a few minutes. Will any of those help you?" ▶ A tutor says, "Do you think you might find it easier to begin with a simpler but similar problem? What might that problem look like?"

Source: Adapted from Fisher and Frey (2014).

Figure 5.3　Types of Cues

TYPE OF CUE	DEFINITION	EXAMPLE
Visual	A range of graphic hints guide students through thinking or understanding.	▶ Highlight places on a text where students have made errors. ▶ Create a graphic organizer to arrange content visually. ▶ Ask students to take a second look at a graphic or visual from a textbook.
Verbal	Variations in speech are used to draw attention to something specific or verbal attention getters that focus students' thinking.	▶ "This is important . . ." ▶ "This is the tricky part. Be careful and be sure to . . ." ▶ Repeat a student's statement using a questioning intonation. ▶ Change volume or speed of speech for emphasis.
Gestural	The tutor's body movements or motions are used to draw attention to something that has been missed.	▶ Make a hand motion that has been taught in advance, such as the one used to indicate the importance of summarizing or predicting while reading. ▶ Place thumbs around a key idea in a text that the student was missing.
Environmental	The surroundings, and items in the surroundings, are used to influence the student's understanding.	▶ Use algebra tiles, magnetic letters, or other manipulatives to guide the student's thinking. ▶ Move an object so that the orientation changes and guides thinking.

Source: Adapted from Fisher and Frey (2014).

Foster Dialogue and Discussion

Teachers who create space for students to pose questions, wrestle with complex issues, clarify thinking, speculate, probe, disagree, resolve problems, and reach consensus are employing a dialogic approach to instruction. This form of instruction assumes a higher level of author-ity on the part of the learner, who co-constructs knowledge under the guidance of a tutor who facilitates the discussion rather than presents information. These conversational teacher moves are intended to help students organize their ideas and ensure productive discussion (Michaels et al., 2016):

Marking conversation	"That's an important point."
Challenging the student	"That's a great question, Rebecca. What do you think?"
Revoicing	"So are you saying that . . . ?"
Asking the student to explain or restate	"Do you disagree or agree, and why?"
Pressing for accuracy	"Can you show me where we can find that information?"
Building on prior knowledge	"How does this connect . . . ?"
Pressing for reasoning	"Why do you think that?"
Expanding reasoning	"Take your time. Say more."
Recapping	"What have you discovered?"

These conversational moves should be punctuated by wait time, both after posing a thought-provoking question (wait time 1) and again after the student responds (wait time 2). The first wait time allows the student to process and contemplate the question, while the second wait time provides the speaker with the space to elaborate on their answer. Ensuring wait time also allows you to process the conversation and results in an increased quality of your questions.

Assess to Check for Understanding

No lesson should occur without gathering and analyzing some form of data to signal what it is that the student currently knows and does not know. These are not isolated measures of a given student's achievement at a single point in time, but rather reveal the overall trajectory of their learning experience. There are two primary ways to assess students' understanding: questioning and writing.

Questioning

The chief way to check for understanding is to ask questions. You're able to glean much more about what a student knows and doesn't know when they respond to a question. In addition to the prompts and dialogic questions discussed previously in this chapter, you can ask the student to explain or summarize a concept or topic. We are listening *to* and listening *for*. Listening *to* a student is the act of locating identity within their utterances. In doing so, we consider how their insights and questions inform us about who they are as an individual. At the same time, we are listening *for* the turns in the conversation that signal content understandings and misconceptions.

Writing

You can also check for understanding through writing. Short writing prompts during the session can allow you to gauge student thinking. These can be used to activate background knowledge, such as asking the student to write a short response to a prompt. "Who was Napoleon and why should we care?" or "Describe the digestive process" or "Why are irrational numbers important in science and engineering?" can be the start of a longer writing piece for them to add to throughout the session.

> *No lesson should occur without gathering and analyzing some form of data.*

Prompts can also be used near the end of the session in the form of an exit slip and should stem from the day's stated learning intention and success criteria. For instance, if the learning intention was to "name four reasons the Pilgrims left England for the New World," then the exit slip should be directly linked. Link the exit slip to a self-assessment by asking the student to rank their level of confidence in their learning:

1. I'm just learning. (I need more help.)

2. I'm almost there. (I need more practice.)

3. I own it! (I can work independently.)

4. I'm a pro! (I can teach others.)

An added benefit is that you now have an actionable plan for what will need to occur in the next session.

These evergreen approaches to lesson design form the core of sound instruction. Having said that, some discipline-specific elements of learning are useful to consider. In the final section of this chapter, we discuss considerations for supporting students in all subject areas as they read texts, learn vocabulary, and write across the curriculum. In addition, we offer some principles for tutoring in mathematics.

Instructional Strategies for Reading

Students often need to read and understand text as a part of your session. However, students who are inefficient readers may not be skilled at *activating their background knowledge*. In addition, they may have difficulty *setting a purpose* for their reading. This second point is crucial for promoting reading comprehension.

> *Anticipation guides encourage students to read with a purpose—to prove or disprove their responses.*

Anticipation Guides

Anticipation guides are used to prepare students for new information by causing them to consider what they know (and do not know) about a topic. These can activate their prior knowledge, encourage predictions, and stimulate curiosity about a topic. To create an anticipation guide, prepare a list of five statements related to the topic of the reading. The statements are true/false or agree/disagree statements designed to engage the student and encourage them to make connections to what they already know. Anticipation guides are useful because students read the text with purpose, to prove or disprove their responses to the statements. They are encouraged to change their responses based on the newly acquired information. A discussion about the statements, questions, and new inquiries should follow the reading. We've created a completed anticipation guide about reading for you in Figure 5.4.

Figure 5.4   Completed Anticipation Guide About Reading

Anticipation Guide for _____

Directions: Read each statement and mark **T** if the statement is true and **F** if the statement is false. Be prepared to explain your reasoning. During and after the reading you may change your responses. Be prepared to explain your responses and use the text for evidence.

TRUE/ FALSE	STATEMENTS	CORRECTED STATEMENTS
F	All readers activate their prior knowledge.	Efficient readers activate their prior knowledge, while struggling readers often need support to do so.
F	All readers think about what they are going to read.	Struggling readers often don't think about the purpose of the text and need to be taught to do so.
T	Effective readers think about what they know and make adjustments while they are reading.	
F	All readers make predictions.	Struggling readers need to be shown how to make predictions.
F	Effective readers delve into reading and read from beginning to end.	No, effective readers use many strategies prior to reading. For example, they predict, make connections, form opinions, and evaluate.

Direct and Intentional Vocabulary Instruction

Develop a reliable routine for teaching targeted vocabulary. Words that are directly taught should not hijack the reading but instead should illuminate it. We like the routine developed by Tennyson and Cocchiarella (1986). We'll use the word *analyze* to demonstrate.

1. **Label and define.** Students first need to be able to attach a short meaning and a label to an unfamiliar word. The teacher might pause to say, "*Analyze* means to look at something carefully so you can solve a problem."

2. **Contextualize.** After defining, ground the word or phrase within the author's use. "I'm going to reread that sentence now. 'The police detective analyzed the crime scene for clues.' Since *analyze* means to look closely to solve a problem, I know he's trying to figure out what happened."

3. **Give a best example.** Link the word to something they might already know. "You've told me about how you use *Fortnite* analysis videos on YouTube to improve your online gaming skills. You're not just watching. You're solving problems to get better at the game."

4. **Elaborate on attributes.** Contrastive examples help the student understand what it is *not*. "When someone is analyzing something, they're breaking it apart into smaller pieces so they can look more closely to understand. A police detective that wasn't looking carefully wouldn't be able to analyze the scene."

5. **Provide strategy information.** Name the strategy you used to figure out the word. "I've heard this word used before on other TV crime shows. So, I thought about how it was used and then made a connection to the story we're reading now."

You can't be a walking dictionary for your students; you must also equip them with the skills they need to solve words on their own. We teach our students a system for figuring out unfamiliar words and phrases they encounter when reading. We ask them to look inside of words and outside of words (Frey & Fisher, 2009).

1. **Look inside the word for structural clues.** Can you break the word apart into chunks? This includes examining to see if there are base or root WORDS along with affixes that reveal further meaning. In addition, you may be able to determine the part of speech. This should begin in the early grades as students learn how smaller units of meaning are combined to make multisyllabic words.

2. **Look outside the word or phrase for contextual clues.** Not all words can be analyzed structurally, but sometimes the author will give you a definition or a synonym that reveals the meaning. A sentence that reads "The house

was cozy, and the people inside were warm and safe" offers context clues to unlock the meaning of *cozy*. Contextual clues come in several forms:

- **Look for antonym or contrast clues.** A word or phrase is clarified using an opposite meaning. "She was brave as she faced her enemy. She would not run away and be labeled a coward."

- **Look for a restatement or synonym clue.** The word or phrase is restated using more common terms. "The police detective discovered that the security guard shirked his duty. The jewelry store was left unprotected when the guard departed before his shift was over."

- **Look for a definition or example clue.** The word or phrase is defined within the sentence. "The science of physiology is the study of how bodies move and function."

3. **When structural and contextual analysis fails, look further outside the word or phrase.** This is when resources should be utilized: dictionaries, glossaries, a quick internet search. Even asking another person is acceptable.

Instructional Strategies for Organizing Ideas and Concepts

Graphic organizers are an instructional strategy to help students visually organize information to support their comprehension. Graphic organizers are useful because they highlight the important ideas in a text and how they are related to one another. They are visual representations of a student's knowledge and are structured to show relationships through labels. Graphic organizers present information in concise ways to show key parts of the whole concept, theme, or topic and are highly effective for all students.

Being actively engaged in processing a text supports comprehension. When students are actively engaged, they are using strategies such as analyzing, synthesizing, evaluating, and summarizing. Graphic organizers help students with these strategies by organizing information to show how it is related. When students use a graphic organizer, they are more likely to become active readers. When graphic organizers correspond with the text structure, they assist the student in clarifying connections and relationships between concepts and ideas found in their reading. Figure 5.5 illustrates four common types of graphic organizers.

Figure 5.5   Four Types of Graphic Organizers

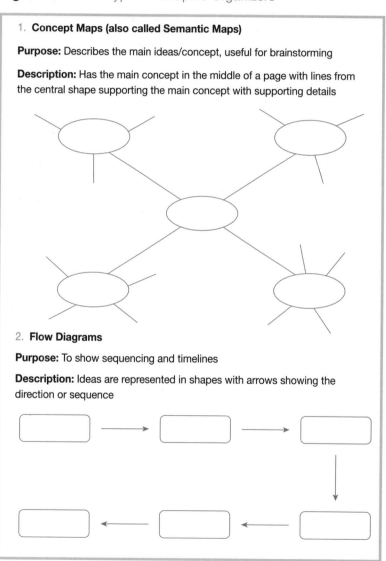

(Continued)

(Continued)

3. Tree Diagrams

Purpose: Used to categorize and classify information; shows relationships and hierarchy

Description: May be horizontal or vertical with lines branching off the main concept into a broad category and lines branching off each category for more detailed information or supporting evidence

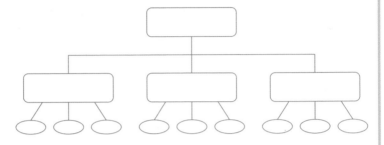

4. Matrices

Purpose: Compare and contrast, shows relationships or classifies attributes

Description: Words or phrases are arranged in a table format horizontally or vertically

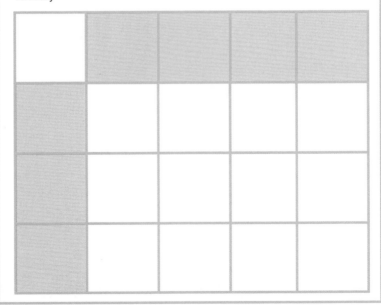

Instructional Strategies for Writing

Students participating in tutoring may be bringing their classroom writing with them for you to use. There can be an expectation on the part of the student that you will "fix it" for them, and then they can go about their day. Or they may have an expectation that they can tell you some things and you'll write it all down for them. The problem with this is that while it may aid the student in the moment, it does little to build their capacity. When they are having trouble getting started, or are not sure how to revise a draft, you can utilize these approaches that teach while providing support.

Students may expect you to "fix" their writing for them.

Parsing the Writing Prompt

Some students have difficulty getting started on a writing assignment and may be meeting with you for writing support. Assistance starts with parsing the writing assignment itself. A well-developed writing assignment should provide the information students need to answer three questions: *What is my purpose for writing this piece? Who is my audience? What is the task?* Students who have trouble getting started may need only to be guided through these three questions to clarify. But for others, it is the thesis statement itself that is the roadblock. They just can't seem to get their heads around a good idea.

Developing Ideas

The development of a central idea or a thesis statement is difficult for many students because, frankly, it requires a lot of thinking. When a student is stuck, the teacher can help by using a sorting activity:

1. Look back through the student's notes and ask them to identify patterns.

2. Ask the student to write one idea or concept on each note. A pad of sticky notes is useful.

3. Help the student to sort these notes into categories.

4. Have the student label the categories.

Often, the student starts drawing conclusions and synthesizing information even before they are finished creating notes. It seems like the physical act of sorting and categorizing brings order to a jumbled mind. This isn't a technique reserved only for novice writers; we often use the same method to organize our writing.

There are times when the sorting activity isn't sufficient, and the student needs further guidance. We use a technique developed by Flower (1993) called *nutshelling*. The aim of nutshelling is to assist struggling writers in distilling their ideas:

1. Students write for several minutes about one of the categories they have developed from the sorting activity and then reread their writing.

2. They then compose one sentence that represents the content of the first round of writing "in a nutshell," so to speak.

3. They write for several more minutes using the nutshell sentence as the first, and then repeat the process.

Leading an individual student through sorting and nutshelling can be time consuming. However, we have witnessed some writers do this for themselves on their own on future writing assignments. The truth is, we all get stuck when writing. Having some techniques for getting yourself unstuck can mean the difference between a blank page and a completed task.

Revising

Unfortunately, in too many classes, revising is just making the changes the teacher recommended during editing, with little thought beyond minimal compliance. ("I'll just make these changes she wrote on my paper, and then I'll be done with this!") But revision is something that ultimately should come from the writer. Start with having the student read aloud what they have written. The act of reading one's words aloud aids them in locating grammatical and syntactic errors they may have overlooked.

> *Start with having the student read aloud what they have written.*

You can also serve as an audience for your student. Use a framework described by Simmons (2003) about three categories of responses that are useful for writers to hear. Begin by reading what they have written and take on the active role of their audience:

1. **Play back the text** for the writer by briefly summarizing the main points as you understood them.

2. **Discuss the reader's needs** by alerting the writer to confusions you had as you read the piece.

3. **Identify the writer's techniques** you noticed, such as the use of headings, examples, and direct quotes.

A responsive reader (you) allows the writer to gain insight into how their words are understood by others. As a writer, it is difficult to distance oneself from one's words, and your response, especially the playback, provides novice writers with a means for hearing their words being interpreted by someone else. We want them to understand that writing is a form of communication that is often understood somewhat differently from what the writer intended. Most important, you want your student to discover that revising is an ongoing process based on the questions posed, the connections made, and the insights shared by audiences.

> *If you review the biographies of major mathematicians, you'll find that the common denominator is that they knew how to struggle.*

Instructional Strategies in Mathematics

A major misconception among many mathematics students (and teachers) is that you have to be talented in order to successfully undertake the subject. Students in math tutoring almost undoubtedly come to your sessions with this notion firmly in place. But if you review the biographies of major mathematicians, you'll find that the common denominator is that they knew how to struggle. They knew that it was not exceptional talent that enabled success but the ability to persist, enjoy the struggle, and see the growth of their learning. Effective math tutors structure their sessions to build the habits and dispositions, not just the skills, of their students.

Exercises Versus Problems

It is important to have a common understanding of the types of mathematics tasks students complete during tutoring. Exercises, which typically make up most of the traditional textbook practice, are provided for students to practice a particular skill, usually devoid of any context. Although these are casually referred to as problems, in reality, they are simply practice exercises.

Problems have context—they are usually written in words that can be situations that apply or provide a context for a mathematical concept. One category of problems is an application that focuses on the use of particular concepts or procedures. Another category of problems is nonroutine or open-ended problems that involve much more than applying a concept or routine.

Engage students in reasoning, exploration, flexible thinking, and making connections during your sessions. Students need deliberate practice, guided by the tutor, not repetitive skill-and-drill tasks. Some tasks should provide students an opportunity to engage in mathematical modeling—taking a problem or situation, representing it mathematically, and doing the mathematics to arrive at a sensible solution or to glean new information that wouldn't have been possible without the mathematics.

Other tasks should require the student to practice applying a concept in different situations. To facilitate strategic thinking, some tasks should be open-ended and have multiple paths to a solution or, in some cases, multiple solutions. Math tasks don't always have to be fun, but they should be interesting and useful.

Math Is Not a Speed Race

Be very careful with timed mathematical tests. Neither fluency nor stamina requires that students work as quickly as possible. Giving students a test that requires them to speed through problems reinforces the idea that they should prioritize doing the "easy" problems first and not spend valuable time on problems that require deeper thinking. Too often, timed tests or speed games are used to check for fluency with basic math facts. The problem is that speed is not part of fluency. Mathematical fluency requires flexible, accurate, and efficient thinking. Fluency also requires a level of conceptual understanding. One would not be considered fluent in a language if they could speak it through mimicry without any comprehension. Students are better served with practice developing fluency rather than racing through written tasks. In addition, speed races cause some students to believe they are not good at math, more likely with students receiving math tutoring. The dispositions students have toward mathematics are important and can impact their willingness to try.

> *Too often, timed tests or speed games are used to check for fluency with basic math facts. The problem is that speed is not part of fluency.*

Conclusion

Sound instructional practices form the core of effective tutoring sessions. They begin with a level of clarity such that students understand what they are learning, why it is important, and what a successful execution will look or sound like. These actions serve as a priming mechanism for the student and hasten learning. Your modeling and thinking aloud about a skill or concept gives students a glimpse into expert decision making. This is coupled with scaffolded instruction and discussion, each key to the kind of dialogic instruction crucial for active learning. These experiences are bracketed with checks for understanding, feedback, and as we will explore in the final chapter, practice. Because texts are often at the center of tutoring across subject areas, it is useful to have instructional tools at your disposal for students to confront vocabulary, conceptual organization, and composition challenges. Tutoring is about capacity-building. After all, you don't want to be doing the vast majority of the reading and writing for them. This is especially the case when it comes to mathematics instruction. Contextualize problems (not exercises) and make sure they see their own progress.

Practice, Deliberately

To improve at anything, we must practice. Some of the learners you partner with need additional time and experiences to capitalize on good instruction. For learners who have experienced instructional loss, reduced instructional minutes, or experienced instruction that may not have worked for them, this practice must be paired with additional teaching. Our model of tutoring relies on opportunities to practice. One of the most essential roles of a tutor is to provide an opportunity for learners to engage in practicing the content, skills, and understandings they need to accelerate their learning.

> *Our model of tutoring relies on opportunities to practice.*

However, not all practice leads to the type of improvement in learning. We are all familiar with the phrase "practice makes perfect." As it turns out, this statement is not entirely true. Not all practice makes perfect, nor is all practice effective at moving learning forward. The more correct phrasing would be "practice makes permanent." Our attention immediately turns to the word *permanent*. There are certain pieces of information, processes, and dispositions that we want our learners to know and do permanently. However, there are also things we do *not* want our learners to permanently know and do. For example, if learners practice something the wrong way (e.g., solving problems, inefficient and effective reading practices), there will be no improvement in learning and quite likely a significant loss of time due to the eventual unlearning and reteaching that must follow this incorrect practice.

So what and how our learners practice is important.

If learners must practice to improve in their learning, what type of practice best supports that improvement when working with a tutor? Let's look at two different learners as they engage with their tutors.

Olivia meets with her tutor three times a week to support her growth in reading. Ms. Dunn is the instructional aide that has been working with Olivia for the year. They have an established routine and Olivia loves working with her at every opportunity.

"All right, Olivia, grab your book and come with me," Ms. Dunn says.

Olivia jumps out of her seat and follows her to a table where they can work together. "Yesterday we stopped at page 7. So find that page and let's get back into this book."

Olivia opens a book she has selected and begins to read aloud. This book is a good fit for her, and she fluently reads as far as she can before her time with Ms. Dunn ends. There are times when she encounters a word or a scenario that requires Ms. Dunn to either tell her the word or explain the situation.

Olivia enjoys her time with Ms. Dunn, and Ms. Dunn loves her role in supporting her reading. Before they both know it, their time together is over, and Olivia heads off to mathematics block.

Like Olivia, Danielle also works with an instructional aide for tutoring in reading. Danielle spends her time with Mr. Lee and has come to enjoy working with him on her reading. Today, Mr. Lee catches Danielle's class returning from the cafeteria. "Hey, Danielle, let's go work on our reading together."

Once in the reading center, Mr. Lee starts the session by saying, "Today we are going to read a piece of text that will challenge our thinking. I am going to read this along with you and we are going to work on understanding the meaning of unfamiliar words and our overall comprehension." Together they review the characteristics of an active reader and strategies for handling words or phrases that they don't know. This piece of text is just outside of her comfort zone.

As Danielle begins to read, it is clear she is challenged by the reading. "I am not sure about this word here," she states. Mr. Lee is quick to coach her through the pronunciation and helps her develop the meaning of the word by looking at the prefix and root word. Then they continue.

Danielle continues to work through the text, rereading when necessary. After some time, Mr. Lee stops her and they spend the next several minutes reviewing the text, focusing on new words, difficult phrases, and comprehension.

Then, off to science block for Danielle.

What are the similarities and differences between these two tutoring examples? In both instances, there is an established relationship that provides the impetus for the students to engage with the tutor and work on their reading. Both Olivia and Danielle appear to have the confidence to take on the task of reading aloud. Finally, both of these young learners have goals for this tutoring session: Olivia is aiming to move farther in her good-fit book and Danielle is aiming to read a challenging piece of text. And this is where the difference lies in these two examples. While each tutoring session involves the learner practicing her reading, the goals and type of practicing are very different.

Two Different Ways to Practice

There are two different kinds of practice: *naïve practice* and *deliberate practice* (Ericsson, 2008; Ericsson & Pool, 2016).

Naïve practice is practice that simply accumulates experience. Because the term *naive* has a very negative connotation, let's simply refer to this type of practice as *repetitive practice*. Typically, repetitive practice is without goals related to moving learning forward, instead focusing on simply increasing the number of hours or experiences with specific content, skills, or understanding. Ericsson et al. (1993) describe learners as simply going through the motions of the task. In our example above, Olivia is remaining in her comfort zone, reading a book that she is already "good at reading," and simply striving to complete the book.

> *There are two different kinds of practice:*
> repetitive practice *and* deliberate practice.

In mathematics, an example of repetitive practice would be learners logging on to an online mathematics platform with their tutor and solving problems that they already know how to solve. Learners are likely going through the motions, simply accumulating the number of hours they practice and the amount of experience they have with, say, place value question. In this case, the role of the tutor is simply to ensure compliance and completion. For science, repetitive practice would be learners repeatedly going over the parts of the nitrogen cycle, going through a deck of digital or paper flashcards that show the steps in cellular respiration, or repeated calculating of the formula weight of different substances. Other examples include writing a word ten times, or one hundred times for that matter, to improve spelling or memorizing dates and facts related to the early explorers in social studies. This says nothing about the relationship between the tutor and the learner or the level of confidence the learner has in taking on these tasks. Instead, this type of practice simply does not move learning forward and underutilizes the potential for the tutor to impact learners, specifically those students who have a damaged relationship with learning.

Now let's look at Danielle's tutoring session through the lens of practice. Danielle is engaged in *deliberate practice*, which has an average effect size of 0.79 (Visible Learning Meta[X], 2021). Deliberate practice, when implemented in a tutoring session, has the potential to double the rate of learning. In deliberate practice, you and the learner

1. Identify a particular area of content, a skill, or essential understanding where additional growth is needed.

2. Use your time together to focus specifically on improving in that particular area of content, a skill, or essential understanding, until it can be integrated into other learning.

Deliberate practice is a mindful and structured way of learning by targeting areas needing acceleration (Ericsson et al., 1993).

> *Deliberate practice, when implemented in a tutoring session, has the potential to double the rate of learning.*

Revisiting the example of Danielle's tutoring session, Mr. Lee has identified two areas that need accelerating: understanding the meaning of unfamiliar words and improving Danielle's overall comprehension of complex text. And, as suggested by Mr. Lee's initial introduction of the tutoring session, this task and the text are outside of Danielle's comfort zone. Finally, Mr. Lee did not simply tell Danielle the answer when she encountered a problem. Instead, he coached her through the challenge to build her capacity for addressing that challenge in the future. This was different from Olivia's experience.

In mathematics, a teacher may recognize that a particular learner struggles with adding and subtracting fractions with unlike denominators. This particular concept and skill would then be an ideal focus for tutoring. Deliberate practice with the tutor could still involve having learners use an online mathematics platform or even playing a game. However, the tasks within that platform or the specific game

Figure 6.1   Two Different Types of Practice in Tutoring

DELIBERATE PRACTICE	NAIVE OR REPETITIVE PRACTICE
Has a specific goal or purpose established by the tutor and the learner beyond accumulating experience or time on task (see Chapter 3)	Has a specific goal or purpose to simply build experience and time on a particular task
Is focused on specific content, skills, and understandings needing additional growth for the learner (see Chapter 5)	Involves the practice of content, skills, and understandings that the learner is already "good at doing"
Pushes learners outside of their comfort zone but is scaffolded and supported by the tutor; the tutor, in this case, acts as a coach (see Chapter 4)	Allows the learner to engage in experiences or tasks that are within their comfort zone
Involves immediate and effective feedback provided by the tutor (see Chapter 2)	Involves immediate and effective feedback; however, the feedback is almost predictable because the learner is already "good at" the experience or task
Can be tailored by the tutor based on the level of challenge and the feedback during the tutoring experience (see Chapter 3)	Is static and not tailored to the specific needs of the learner

should be chosen intentionally to target this area of need and should focus on developing learning strategies for approaching fractions with unlike denominators in the near and distant future. If a learner found multistep contextualized problems confusing, deliberate practice might involve you and the learner acting out, sketching, visualizing, and talking out similar problems to make sense of them but not worry about actually solving them yet; thus, your time together with the learner focuses on the targeted area of need in a very deliberate way.

In science, a teacher may see that her learners are having considerable difficulty in metric conversions, especially in units of energy, force, and momentum. When with the tutor, learners would devote their time to engaging in conversions that were at the right level of challenge, but with immediate and effective feedback and continuous adjustments to the tasks based on that feedback.

For spelling, deliberate practice might involve repeated spelling "tests" in which the learner, alongside their tutor, analyzes the location in the word where the error occurred and then focuses the learning on that spelling pattern, generalizing to other words with a similar pattern (to note, we recognize that not all words used in language work this way).

If a learner encountered challenges remembering the differences between Athens and Sparta (or the French, Russian, American, and Glorious Revolutions), deliberate practice with the tutor would focus on building the capacity in the learning in this particular content. Deliberate practice can involve both learning the content as well as learning how to learn. For Athens and Sparta, the deliberate practice may focus on identifying and using tools for comparing/contrasting in social studies (e.g., graphic organizer, thinking map, concept map).

Components of Deliberate Practice

Deliberate practice is required to move individuals beyond everyday skills and toward mastery and proficiency in content, skills, and understandings (Ericsson, 2006). Figure 6.2 shows a learner's trajectory based on two different types of practice.

Figure 6.2 Learning Trajectories for Different Types of Practice

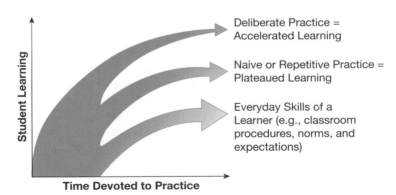

Source: Adapted from Ericsson (2006).

To understand how to leverage deliberate practice during your time with learners, we will unpack the specific components that must be present in deliberate practice. In other words, how can you, as an essential part in the acceleration of student learning, advocate for and engage learners in deliberate practice?

Deliberate practice involves five key components that separate this type of practice from repetitive or naive practice, emphasizing *quality* over quantity (Ericsson & Pool, 2016).

Five Components of Deliberate Practice

1. Individuals engage in an exercise, task, or experience outside of their current skill level.

2. The exercise, task, or experience is focused on a specific and measurable learning or performance goal.

3. The environment of the practice allows for the individual to focus on the exercise, task, or experience.

4. The individual receives effective feedback.

5. A mental model is developed that allows the individual to self-regulate future performance.

To accelerate student learning, tutors can provide both opportunities and an environment that allows for the deliberate practice of learners. This compels teachers, learners, and their tutors to use a shared language of learning and clear expectations, have multiple opportunities to engage in formative checks for understanding, identify areas of growth, develop goals for improvement, receive effective feedback on their progress toward their goals, and develop learning strategies for integrating this learning into future content, skills, and understandings. Figure 6.3 presents specific actions you can take in partnering with teachers and learners.

Figure 6.3   Deliberate Practice and Tutoring

COMPONENTS OF DELIBERATE PRACTICE	ACTIONS FOR DEVELOPING EXPERTISE IN TEACHING
Individuals engage in an exercise, task, or experience outside of their current skill level.	Tutors must collaborate with classroom teachers to gain clarity around areas for growth in content and skills; this clarity should pull from the standards of learning, the learner's prior growth and achievement data, and general observations of the student engaged in learning.
The exercise, task, or experience is focused on a specific and measurable learning or performance goal.	Tutors, alongside classroom teachers and the learner, should extract specific goals for each tutoring session. These goals should be specific, measurable, and appropriate for the tutoring session.
The environment of the practice allows for the individual to focus on the exercise, task, or experience.	Tutoring sessions should not take place in the cafeteria, hallway, or the back of the classroom. Learners must have time, space, and resources in an area that does not distract them from their learning.
The individual receives effective feedback.	During the tutoring session, use observations, student conversations, and work samples to provide immediate and constant feedback. In addition, the tutor should adjust the next steps in the session based on that feedback.
A mental model is developed that allows the individual to self-regulate future performance.	The tutor should scaffold the feedback to allow for the development of self-reflection, self-monitoring, and self-evaluating of teaching and learning. In other words, support the learners as they learn how to learn.

Deliberate Practice in Action

Micah is an eighth-grade algebra student at Forest Lakes Middle School. While he was tapped to enroll in Algebra I as an eighth grader, he has struggled to make progress this year as he has in prior years.

"I have always enjoyed math and been good at math until I got to this class." What is most notable is that his attitude and dispositions toward mathematics in general are shifting. "Maybe I am not good at math anymore."

His teacher, Lee Ann Whitesell, recognizes that his relationship with mathematics and learning has taken a huge hit this year. She quickly points out that "there are several skills that he must work on and a few big ideas that will allow him to connect the dots. Once that happens, he will take off in this class and his subsequent math classes."

The principal at Forest Lakes Middle School has decided to use available resources to offer tutoring to students who need additional scaffolding and support. "We have spent time providing professional learning to a cadre of retired teachers, paraprofessionals, and volunteers to tutor in mathematics, an area of focus in our strategic plan," Ms. Larson shares. "Al Samuels, a retired mathematics teacher, has been matched with Micah. They have established a strong relationship and Mr. Samuels has increased Micah's confidence in math. It is back to where he was in seventh grade."

Let's see how deliberate practice is put into action during Micah and Mr. Samuels' tutoring sessions. Before the next tutoring session, Mr. Samuels, who Micah now refers to as "Al," met with Ms. Whitesell to isolate the specific skills and concepts Micah needs to work on. These specific skills and concepts must align with the specific learning targets in the classroom as well as the specific standards of learning. However, we must point out that identifying these typically falls on the classroom teacher, as it is unreasonable to ask a tutor to unpack standards.

Deliberate Practice in Action Step 1: Isolate the skill or concept that needs attention during tutoring.

From there, Al has to decide if he will draw from the observations and work samples offered by Ms. Whitesell or engage Micah in a learning experience or task that allows him to identify his prior knowledge and skills around the specific skills or concepts.

Deliberate Practice in Action Step 2: Identify prior knowledge and understanding.

For you, this part of the process will depend on your comfort level with the content. Had Al not been a retired mathematics teacher, this would have been the ideal opportunity to collaborate further with Ms. Whitesell. There is nothing wrong with gaining this information from the classroom teacher. However you feel most comfortable, make sure to have a starting point for the student's learning progression.

The teacher will have evidence of the learner's prior knowledge and understanding. As the tutor, you have the awesome opportunity to spend uninterrupted, individual time with this learner and gather your evidence of what the learner already knows, understands, and is able to do. If you do decide to gather your observations and work samples, sharing and analyzing them with the classroom teacher allows for the two of you to triangulate evidence of learning and gain a better understanding of how to best accelerate this student's learning.

Deliberate Practice in Action Step 3: Set an individual goal for the tutoring session.

The combining of the specific skill, concept, and prior knowledge and understanding allows Al to decide where to focus the deliberate practice during the tutoring session. For example, "We are going to work on his conceptual understanding of what a solution is to a system of equations. Today is going to be conceptual, but with problems and scenarios he has never seen before."

From there, Al draws from the mathematics textbook, online resources, and his own experiences to find problems and scenarios outside of Micah's comfort zone.

Deliberate Practice in Action Step 4: Design the practice experience or task for the tutoring session.

Notice that the implication here is that Al has access to resources that allow him to both set an individual goal and plan the experience or task. As a tutor, this may not be the case for you. Again, partnering with the classroom teacher, instructional coach, and other individuals in the school is important in ensuring that the practice is deliberate.

Deliberate Practice in Action Step 5: Reevaluate knowledge and understanding.

Finally, the experience or task must generate evidence of Micah's learning so that Al can both provide feedback and make adjustments "on the spot" in the tutoring session.

"When our time is up, Al always lets me know where we are going next. I like how he tells me what we will work on next time. It helps me relax and be comfortable in class with Ms. Whitesell. I know I will get the help I need."

Figure 6.4   Deliberate Practice in Action

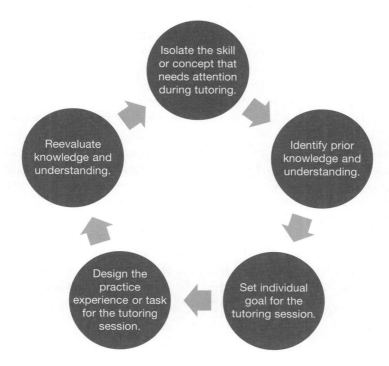

Conclusion

Getting learners to practice is quite a challenge. Whether in the primary or secondary classroom, the menu of options that distract them from practice is endless. In the past, homework has been our attempt to encourage, coerce, and even force learners to practice. That has yielded less than impressive results and a whole lot of controversy. However, leveraging the access and skills of a tutor lessens this challenge. Tutoring is an approach that can accelerate learning by partnering students with someone with whom they can

▌ Establish a nurturing relationship.

▌ Build confidence in the learning and approach challenges with that confidence.

▌ Set learning goals that focus on their learning needs.

▌ Build their capacity as self-regulated learners.

▌ Build their knowledge, skills, and understanding around what they need to know to be successful now and in the future.

▌ Be deliberate in their practicing of essential knowledge, skills, and understanding.

How we leverage the skills of a tutor through that last bulleted point, practice, makes all the difference in the tutoring model.

Let us be clear. There is a place for naive or repetitive practice. We participate in recreational sports and activities where our goal is simply to enjoy the time. Thus, developing enough confidence and competence to do just that is just fine. In our classrooms, there are everyday skills associated with classroom processes, protocols, and norms where repetitive practice is all that is needed. Again, that is just fine. But our focus over the past several chapters is not on these everyday recreational activities or everyday classroom skills. Our focus is on accelerating student learning, something for which there is no substitute in its value and importance to the success of our learners. We must have higher expectations for the actualized learning potential of our students than we do for recreational activities and everyday skills—especially for learners who have a damaged relationship with learning. The potential to have an impact on students, accelerating their learning in a way that leaves them with the skills to drive their own learning in the future, is of paramount importance. The deliberate practice of learning converts this potential into impact, and you, as a tutor, play a vital role.

References

Adler, M. J., & Van Doren, C. L. (1972). *How to read a book.* Touchstone.

Bracken, B. A. (1996). *Handbook of self-concept: Developmental, social, and clinical considerations.* John Wiley & Sons.

CALM. (n.d.). *10 ways to nurture your child's self concept.* https://calm4kids.org/10-ways-to-nurture-your-childs-self-concept

Chew, S. L., & Cerbin, W. J. (2020). The cognitive challenges of effective teaching. *The Journal of Economic Education, 52*(1), 17–40. https://doi.org/10.1080/00220485.2020.1845266

Cornelius-White, J. (2007). Learner-centered teacher–student relationships are effective: A meta-analysis. *Review of Educational Research, 77,* 113–143.

Costello, B., Wachtel, J., & Wachtel, T. (2009). *Restorative practices handbook for teachers, disciplinarians, and administrators.* International Institute for Restorative Practices.

Dweck, C. S. (2006). *Mindset: The new psychology of success.* Ballantine.

Eanes, R. (n.d.). Parenting: 10 ways to nurture your child's self-concept. *Creative Child.* https://www.creativechild.com/articles/view/parenting-10-ways-to-nurture-your-childs-self-concept

Eccles, J. S. (2009). Who am I and what am I going to do with my life? Personal and collective identities as motivators of action. *Educational Psychologist, 44*(2), 78–89.

Eckert, D. (2019, September 4). Curious kids: Why are some people affected by sleep paralysis? *The Conversation.* https://theconversation.com/curious-kids-why-are-some-people-affected-by-sleep-paralysis-121125

Ericsson, K. A. (2006). The influence of experience and deliberate practice on the development of superior expert performance. In K. A. Ericsson, N. Charness, P. J. Feltovich, & R. R. Hoffman (Eds), *The Cambridge handbook of expertise and expert performance* (pp. 683–703). Cambridge University Press.

Ericsson, K. A. (2008). Deliberate practice and acquisition of expert performance: A general overview. *Academic Emergency Medicine, 15*(11), 988–994.

Ericsson, K. A., Krampe, R. T., & Tesch-Romer, C. (1993). The role of deliberate practice in the acquisition of expert performance. *Psychological Review, 100*(3), 363–406.

Ericsson, K. A., & Pool, R. (2016). *Peak. Secrets from the new science of expertise*. Houghton Mifflin Harcourt.

Fendick, F. (1990). *The correlation between teacher clarity of communication and student achievement gain: A meta-analysis* [Unpublished doctoral dissertation]. University of Florida, Gainesville.

Fisher, D., & Frey, N. (2014). *Better learning through structured teaching: A framework for the gradual release of responsibility* (2nd ed.). ASCD.

Fisher, D., Frey, N., Bustamante, V., & Hattie, J. (2021). *The assessment playbook for distance and blended learning*. Corwin.

Fisher, D., Frey, N., & Hattie, J. (2016). *Visible learning for literacy, K–12*. Corwin.

Fisher, D., Frey, N., & Hattie, J. (2017). *Teaching literacy in the visible learning classroom, grades K–5*. Corwin.

Fisher, D., Frey, N., Hattie, J., & Flories, K. (2019a). *Becoming an assessment-capable visible learner, grades 3–5: Learner's notebook*. Corwin.

Fisher, D., Frey, N., Hattie, J., & Flories, K. (2019b). *Becoming an assessment-capable visible learner, grades 6–12: Learner's notebook*. Corwin.

Fisher, D., Frey, N., & Smith, D. (2020). *The teacher credibility and collective efficacy playbook, grades K–12*. Corwin.

Flower, L. (1990). Negotiating academic discourse. In L. Flower, V. Stein, J. Ackerman, M. J. Kantz, K. McCormick, & W. C. Peck (Eds.), *Reading-to-write: Exploring a cognitive and social process* (pp. 221–252). Oxford University Press.

Flower, L. (1993). *Problem-solving strategies for writing* (4th ed.). Harcourt Brace College.

Frey, N., & Fisher, D. (2009). *Learning words inside and out: Vocabulary instruction that boosts achievement in all subject areas*. Heinemann.

Frey, N., Hattie, J., & Fisher, D. (2018). *Developing assessment-capable learners: Maximizing skill, will, and thrill*. Corwin.

Gordon, T. (2003). *Teacher effectiveness training: The program proven to help teachers bring out the best in students of all ages*. Three Rivers Press.

Guthrie, J. T., Hoa, A. L. W., Wigfield, A., Tonks, S. M., Humenick, N. M., & Littles, E. (2007). Reading motivation and reading comprehension growth in the later elementary years. *Contemporary Educational Psychology, 32*(3), 282–313.

Hattie, J. (2018). *250 influences chart*. Retrieved from https://www.visiblelearning.com/content/visible-learning-research

Hattie, J., & Timperley, H. (2007). The power of feedback. *Review of Educational Research, 77*(1), 81–112.

Hattie, J., & Zierer, K. (2018). *10 mindframes for Visible Learning: Teaching for success*. Routledge.

Hoy, W. K., & Tschannen-Moran, M. (2003). The conceptualization and measurement of faculty trust in schools. In W. Hoy & C. Miskel (Eds.), *Studies in leading and organizing schools* (pp. 181–208). Greenwich, CT: Information Age Publishing.

Hughes, G., Wood, E., & Kitagawa, K. (2014). Use of self-referential (ipsative) feedback to motivate and guide distance learners. *Open Learning, 29*(1), 31–44. https://doi.org/10.1080/02680513.2014.921612

Isaacs, T., Zara, C., Herbert, G., Coombs, S. J., & Smith, C. (2013). Ipsative assessment. In T. Isaacs, C. Zara, G. Herbert, S. J. Coombs, & C. Smith, *The SAGE Key Concepts Series: Key concepts in educational assessment* (pp. 80–82). SAGE.

Kapur, M. (2019, September 28). Productive failure. *TEDx Lugano.* https://www.manukapur.com/prof-manu-kapur-at-tedx-lugano-sep-28-2019

Martin, A. J. (2006). Personal bests (PBs): A proposed multidimensional model and empirical analysis. *British Journal of Educational Psychology, 76,* 803-825

Martin, A. J. (2011). Personal best (PB) approaches to academic development: Implications for motivation and assessment. *Educational Practice and Theory, 33,* 93–99.

Mehrabian, A. (1971). *Silent messages.* Wadsworth.

Michaels, S., O'Connor, M. C., Hall, M. W., & Resnick, L. B. (2016). Accountable Talk® sourcebook: For classroom conversation that works. *University of Pittsburgh Institute for Learning.* https://ifl.pitt.edu/documents/AT-SOURCEBOOK2016.pdf

Nuthall, G. (2007). *The hidden lives of learners.* NZCER Press.

Palmer, D. H., Dixon, J., & Archer, J. (2016). Identifying underlying causes of situational interest in a science course for preservice elementary teachers. *Science Education, 100*(6), 1039–1061.

Pauk, W., & Owens, R. J. Q. (2010). *How to study in college* (10th ed.). Wadsworth/Cengage Learning.

Paul, R. (1995). *The art of redesigning instruction* [Technical report]. Foundation for Critical Thinking.

Poe, E. A. (1988). *Marginalia.* Charlottesville: University of Virginia. (Original work published 1844)

Priniski, S. J., Hecht, C. A., & Harackiewicz, J. M. (2018). Making learning personally meaningful: A new framework for relevance research. *Journal of Experimental Education, 86*(1), 11–29.

Rogers, C. A. (1959). Theory of therapy, personality, and interpersonal relationships as developed in the client-centered framework. In S. Koch (Ed.), *Psychology: A study of a science. Vol. 3: Formulations of the person and the social context.* McGraw-Hill.

Rollins, S. P. (2014). *Learning in the fast lane.* ASCD.

Shulman, L. S. (1986). Those who understand: Knowledge growth in teaching. *Educational Researcher, 15*(2), 4–14.

Simmons, J. (2003). Responders are taught, not born. *Journal of Adolescent and Adult Literacy, 46*(8), 684–693.

Slavin, R. (2018). New findings on tutoring: Four shockers. *Robert Slavin's Blog*. https://robertslavinsblog.wordpress.com/2018/04/05/new-findings-on-tutoring-four-shockers

Tennyson, R. D., & Cocchiarella, M. J. (1986). An empirically based instructional design theory for teaching concepts. *Review of Educational Research, 56*(1), 40–71.

Tomkins, S. S. (1962). *Affect imagery consciousness: The positive affects.* Springer.

Visible Learning Meta[X]. (2021, April). www.visiblelearningmetax.com

von Frank, V. (2010). Trust matters—for educators, parents, and students. *Tools for Schools, 14*(1), 1–3.

Wabisabi Learning. (n.d.). *6 ways of building student confidence through your practice.* wabisabilearning.com/blogs/mindfulness-wellbeing/building-student-confidence-6-ways

Won, S., Lee, S. Y., & Bong, M. (2017). Social persuasions by teachers as a source of student self-efficacy: The moderating role of perceived teacher credibility. *Psychology in the Schools, 54*(5), 532–547.

Index

About the Authors

Nancy Frey, PhD, is a professor in educational leadership at San Diego State University and a leader at Health Sciences High and Middle College. She has been a special education teacher, reading specialist, and administrator in public schools. Nancy has engaged in professional learning communities as a member and in designing schoolwide systems to improve teaching and learning for all students. She has published numerous books, including *The Teacher Clarity Playbook* and *Rigorous Reading*.

Douglas Fisher, PhD, is a professor of educational leadership at San Diego State University and a leader at Health Sciences High and Middle College. He has served as a teacher, language development specialist, and administrator in public schools and nonprofit organizations, including eight years as the Director of Professional Development for the City Heights Collaborative, a time of increased student achievement in some of San Diego's urban schools. Doug has engaged in professional learning communities for several decades, building teams that design and implement systems to impact teaching and learning. He has published numerous books on teaching and learning, such as *Assessment-Capable Visible Learners* and *Engagement by Design*.

John Almarode, PhD, is an associate professor and executive director of teaching and learning in the College of Education at James Madison University (JMU). He has worked with schools, classrooms, and teachers all over the world and has presented locally, nationally, and internationally on the application of the science of learning to the classroom, school, and home environments. At JMU, he works with preservice teachers and actively pursues his research interests, including the science of learning and the design and measurement of classroom environments that promote student engagement and learning. John has authored multiple articles, reports, book chapters, and over a dozen books on effective teaching and learning in today's schools and classrooms.

A SAGE Publishing Company

Helping educators make the greatest impact

CORWIN HAS ONE MISSION: to enhance education through intentional professional learning.

We build long-term relationships with our authors, educators, clients, and associations who partner with us to develop and continuously improve the best evidence-based practices that establish and support lifelong learning.

> ## Every student deserves a great teacher— not by chance, but by design.

Read more from Fisher & Frey

Catapult teachers beyond learning intentions to define clearly what success looks like for every student. Designed to be used collaboratively in grade-level, subject-area teams—or even on your own—this step-by-step playbook expands teacher understanding of how success criteria can be utilized to maximize student learning.

Disrupt the cycle of implicit bias and stereotype threat with 40 research-based, teacher-tested techniques; individual, classroom-based, and schoolwide actions; printables; and ready-to-go tools for planning and instruction.

Explore a new model of reading instruction that goes beyond teaching skills to fostering engagement and motivation. *Comprehension* is the structured framework you need to empower students to comprehend text and take action in the world.

When you increase your credibility with students, student motivation rises. And when you partner with other teachers to achieve this, students learn more. This playbook illuminates the connection between teacher credibility and collective efficacy and offers specific actions educators can take to improve both.

Tap your intuition, collaborate with your peers, and put the research-based strategies embedded in this road map to work in your classroom to implement or deepen a strong, successful balanced literacy program.

With cross-curricular examples, planning templates, professional learning questions, and a PLC guide, this is the most practical planner for designing and delivering highly effective instruction.

To order your copies, visit corwin.com/FisherandFrey